CONIECTANEA BIBLICA • NEW TESTAMENT SERIES 25

EVALD LÖVESTAM

Jesus and 'this Generation'

A New Testament Study

Almqvist & Wiksell International, Stockholm
1995

Translated by Moira Linnarud

Abstract

Lövestam, O. Evald, Jesus and 'this Generation'. A New Testament Study. Coniectanea Biblica. New Testament Series 25, Lund 1995. 130 pp. Monograph. ISBN 91-
22-01668-6.

In this book the term 'this generation' ('this *genea*') in the New Testament is
discussed. It is almost entirely to be found in the Synoptics and there, without
exception, in the words of Jesus. Here it is investigated against the background of
relevant expressions and concepts in ancient Israel. The different New Testament
passages where the phrase is found are thoroughly penetrated from this perspective. It
is shown that the terminology in question has a significant meaning which sheds light
on a variety of texts. As a recurrent expression on the lips of Jesus it also contributes to
our understanding of how Jesus looked on himself and his mission.

Published with grants from The Swedish Council for Research in the Humanities and
Social Sciences.

Printed by Wallin & Dalholm, Lund   ISBN 91-22-01668-6

Content

Introduction

In the synoptic Gospels, Jesus uses the phrase ἡ γενεὰ αὕτη several times and in different contexts. It is found in his answer to the demand for a sign, in his parable of the playing children, in his words of judgement in Mt 23:29–36 par., in his statement that 'this *genea*' will not pass away until the prophesied eschatological events take place, etc. Apart from the Synoptics, the term occurs only once in Acts and besides that in the Old Testament references in Heb 3:10 and Phil 2:15 ('a *genea*'). What does this expression really imply? What are its meaning and function on the lips of Jesus? This study gives a comprehensive treatment of the New Testament text material on the theme.

The Greek phrase obviously has a Semitic basis. It is thus natural to start in the Old Testament and the post-biblical Jewish literature to see if the terminology has its origins there. The answer is in the affirmative. It appears that the phrase has its background in an early Israelitic way of expression and pattern of thought to which a many-facetted complex of ideas was associated. With this starting point, the task is to penetrate the different 'this *genea*' passages in the New Testament with the purpose of thus trying to reach the significant meaning of the expression and an adequate understanding of the relevant texts. The results of that quest justify pursuing the question if the terminology in the mouth of Jesus has not in fact something significant to tell us about his self-understanding, a matter which is briefly discussed in an Epilogue. Finally, in an Appendix it is shown how the argumentation in 2 Pet 3:3-13 is related to the complex of ideas associated with the term, with consequences for our understanding of the passage.

In the title, the Greek phrase ἡ γενεὰ αὕτη is rendered by 'this generation' in accordance with the praxis in English translations of the New Testament.

1. An early Jewish Perspective

Within the framework of the New Testament use of the word γενεά, the phrase ἡ γενεὰ αὕτη is a recurrent expression. It is to be found almost exclusively in the Synoptics.[1] The form can vary somewhat. Often one or more censorious adjectives are added to γενεά: πονηρός, μοιχαλίς and others. On occasion αὕτη can also be missing, e.g. Mark 9:19: ὦ γενεὰ ἄπιστος (καὶ διεστραμμένη). There is, however, no mistaking the generally uniform use of the term. In fact it has almost the character of a *terminus technicus*.[2]

As to its meaning in New Testament contexts, it can, to start with, be established that Greek ἡ γενεὰ αὕτη renders Hebr הַדּוֹר הַזֶּה.[3] That would imply that the concept has its roots in the Old Testament/early Jewish world of ideas. This point will be developed further later. Here reference will only be made to the fact that the pejorative adjectives associated with γενεά almost all relate back to Old Testament sayings, especially Deut 32:5,20 (cf. Deut 1:35): ἄπιστος (Mk 9:19 - Deut 32:20b), ἄπιστος καὶ διεστραμμένη (Mt 17:17 par. Lk 9:41 - Deut 32:5 compared with 32:20b), σκολιός (Acts 2:40 - Deut 32:5), πονηρός (Mt 12:39 par. Lk 11:29; Mt 16:4 - Deut 1:35, MT), ἀμαρτωλός (Mk 8:38 - Deut 32:5a compared with Deut 32:5b).[4]

The word דּוֹר shows considerable variation in its purport. It can have varied references. In the Old Testament it is mostly used of 'generation' in the true sense. But it is also used of דור צדיק, the *dor* of the righteous (in contrast to the evildoers, Ps 14:5), of דור אבותיו, his fathers' *dor* (i.e. the dead, Ps 49:20), of דור בניך, that is the *dor* of God's children (Ps 73:15), of דור ישרים, the *dor* of the upright (Ps 112:2), of דר רישון, the former *dor* (generally seen, Job 8:8), etc.[5]

---

[1] There is an exception in Acts 2:40; moreover the term occurs in the Old Testament quotation in Heb 3:7–11 (v. 10; cf. Phil 2:15 where αὕτη is missing).

[2] Cf. M. Meinertz, "'Dieses Geschlecht' im Neuen Testament", *BZ* NF 1 (1957), 285; A. Polag, *Die Christologie der Logienquelle*, 1977, 138.

[3] Cf. *BDR* § 292 n. 4.

[4] In Phil 2:15 the allusion to Dt 32:5 is clear.

[5] The etymology of דּוֹר is uncertain; it is possible that the word is etymologically related to the concept of 'circle', and this is then a basis for its varying use. See G.J. Botterweck, s.v. דּוֹר in *TWAT* II, with references. For other suggestions as to etymology, see e.g. G. Gerleman s.v. דּוֹר in *THAT* I, with references. In the context here it is not decisive how the question of the etymology of the word is answered. It

In post-biblical Jewish scriptures the variation in the meaning of the term is just as substantial. Even here דּוֹר usually means 'generation' in the true sense, but, just as in the Old Testament, the word can frequently have other meanings. It is not unusual that the criteria for the definition of the term are particular qualifications and characteristics in the one case or the other. These qualifications and characteristics can e.g. be connected to a single prominent individual, a number of prominent individuals, a significant event, a particular historical situation.

Within the framework of the use of the word in early Jewish literature there exist some expressions which are of interest from the aspect of the New Testament. Such an expression is 'the *dor* of the Messiah'. In Ex 17:16 it says e.g. that the Lord will be at war with Amalek מדר דר 'from generation to generation'. In *Mek.* Ex ad loc. R. Joshua (c. 90 AD) assigns MT:s מדר דר to the life of this world and the life of the world to come.[6] The Palestinian Targum of that passage gives the following paraphrase: מדרא דעלמא דין ומדרא דמשיחא ומדרא דעלמא דאתי 'from the *dara'* of this world, from the *dara'* of the Messiah, and from the *dara'* of the world to come'. Here this age's *dor* and the coming age's *dor* are expressly mentioned, and between them comes the *dor* of the Messiah. That is a recurrent concept in ancient Judaism.[7] With the era of the Messiah in view, *Pss. Sol.* 18 talks e.g. about the good which the Lord will do γενεᾷ τῇ ἐρχομένῃ 'for the *genea* that is to come' (v. 6); and later, the people of the Messianic kingdom are characterised as γενεὰ ἀγαθὴ ἐν φόβῳ θεοῦ ἐν ἡμέραις ἐλέους 'a good *genea* in the fear of God in the days of mercy' (v.9).[8] Among the rabbis there were quite varied opinions as to the length of the Messianic age, ranging from forty to several thousand years.[9] The term דור in the expression דורו של משיח does not imply any

should, however, be stated that דּוֹר unlike γενεά does not belong to the same category as conception, birth and descent.

[6] Cf. Philo's use of the Greek γενεά to refer to the human race before and after the Flood when he says that Noah was both the end of the condemned *genea* and the beginning of the blameless one; *De praemis et poenis* 23.

[7] See e.g. *Sipre Deut.* § 310 (134a); *Midr. Ps* 2 § 9 (14b); 16 § 4 (61a); *Cant. Rab.* 6:10 § 1 (34b); *Pesiq. Rab Kah.* 29a; *Pesiq. R.*36 (161b); *b. Sanh.* 99a.

[8] Cf. Schüpphaus, *Die Psalmen Salomos*, 1977, 74. Cf. how the eschatalogical congregation is called 'a generation of righteousness' (γενεὰ δικαιοσύνης) in *1 Enoch* 107:1.

[9] See e.g. P. Volz, *Die Eschatologie der jüdischen Gemeinde*, 1934, 226-228; E. Schürer, *The History of the Jewish People in the Age of Jesus Christ* II, 1979, 523 f.; 536 f. - The matter of the relationship between the present age, the days of the Messiah, and the future age and the rabbis' change of opinion on this matter will not be gone into in this context. See Str-B IV, 799-976.

determination in this respect; according to a statement which recurs in several places, the דור of the Messiah consists of three דורות.[10] של דורו משיח simply refers to the Messianic people without defining the extent of the age in time. The concept 'the *dor* of the Messiah' is not without importance from the perspective of the New Testament.[11] The phrase 'this *dor/genea*' in the New Testament texts cannot, however, primarily be connected to it with its positive connotations. What is meant there is not 'a good *genea* in the fear of God' but a *genea* with negative characteristics.

Another interesting concept in this connection is that of the last *dor/genea*. In the Dead Sea Scrolls in particular, it is used in a way that is worthy of attention. In these texts the phrase הדור האחרון 'the final *dor*' occurs several times.[12] In CD 1:12 דור אחרון is assumed to be an evil *dor*.[13] It is described more closely as עדה בוגדים, i.e. the congregation of those who betray God and turn aside from his way.[14] The sayings in 1QpHab 2:6 f. and 7:1 ff. are not least interesting in this context. They speak about what is to come upon הדור האחרון 'the final *dor*', the length of which is, however, not specified. The final age will be prolonged and its end has not been made known by God. These texts have been referred to primarily in the interpretations of Mk 13:30,32 with its parallels – and rightly so, from some points of view.[15] The vital background information on the 'this *genea*' terminology in the New Testament is, however, not to be found here either.

To be able to trace this background it is important to bear in mind the fact that the phrase in its New Testament contexts has generally definite negative connotations. Further, that the adjectives used clearly point to the Old Testament and there mainly relate to expressions about the rebellious and faithless *dor* of the 'first exodus'.[16] It is then an essential task to study more closely the thoughts

---

[10] This statement is often assigned to R. Jose (c. 100 AD); e.g. in *Tanch.* (ed. Buber) חצא § 18 (22b-23a); *Pesiq. Rab Kah.* 29a. In *Mek.* Ex 17:16 it is traced to R. Eliezer (c. 90 AD). In this description of the duration of the *dor* of the Messiah there is regular reference to the expression דור דורים in Ps 72:5, interpreted according to the principle that a plural refers to no less than two, and one *dor* + two *dorot* makes three *dorot*.

[11] In its context the words quoted in Acts 8:33: "who can describe his *genea*?" apparently refer to the Messianic *dor/genea*.

[12] Apart from the passages below, see also 1QpMicah 17-19; cf. 4QpHos[b] 1:11: דור] אח[ר]ית.

[13] Cf. 4QpHos[b] 1:10: דור הפקדה, the '*dor* of Visitation'.

[14] Cf. 1QSb 3:7: דור עלה[ה] 'a *dor* of wickedness'.

[15] See below chap. 8.

and ideas which were associated with דור המדבר 'the *dor* of the Wilderness' in old Jewish times and other concepts of that kind that can have relevance in this context. There דור המדבר was a *dor* which was often mentioned together with other *dorot* and collectives in the history of the world and Israel: 'Enoch's דור' which was associated with idol worship (Gen 4:26 according to *Tg. Neof.*, e.g.) and for whose sake a third of the world is said to have been struck by floods[17], 'the דור of the Flood', 'the דור of the Dispersion' (at the Tower of Babel), 'the men of Sodom', etc.[18]

As will be seen in the following, there is reason to pay special attention to דור המבול 'the *dor* of the Flood' as well as דור המדבר 'the *dor* of the Wilderness', regarding background material for the terminology of 'this *genea*' in the New Testament.[19]

References to the collective that was struck by the punishment of the Flood are frequent in early Jewish scriptures.[20] The theme was a highly relevant one. The fate of those who had lived in disbelief and sin before the Flood served as a warning for people of later times.

דור המבול is described as deeply wicked, and its wickedness is sometimes traced all the way back to Cain's murder of his brother; for Cain's sake the earth was drowning in a flood.[21] It is more common, however, that it is traced back to the 'sons of God' and their relationship with the daughters of men in Gen 6:2 f. This is the view in CD 2:18-21. In *1 Enoch* it is described how 'the sons of God' were responsible for the spread of disobedience, lawlessness and injustice throughout the world (chapter 7-9). Therefore judgement was passed: The whole earth would be destroyed, and a deluge was about to come upon the whole earth, and would destroy all that was on it (10:2,9,15[22]; cf. *Jub.* 5:1-5). The same

---

16 Above p. 8 and below p. 21 f. and passim

17 *Mek.* Ex 20:3; *Sipre Deut.* 43 (81b) etc.

18 These *dorot* and collectives are mentioned together - greater or lesser numbers of them - in *m. Sanh.*10 (11):3; *Mek.* Ex 15:1; *Gen. Rab.* 2:3 (12a); 28:2 (59b); 30:9 (63a); 38:6 (77a); *Lev. Rab.* 23:3 (33a); 23:9 (33b); *Sipre Deut.* § 311 (134a); 318 (136a); *Midr. Ps.* 1 § 12–14 (6a–7b) and in many other places. Cf. Sir 16:7-10. - NB Josephus' saying in *Bell.* V § 566: If the Romans had delayed the destruction of Jerusalem any longer, "either the earth would have opened and swallowed up the city (i.e. like Korah and his company, Num 16:32), or it would have been swept away by a flood (i.e. like the *dor* of the Flood), or have tasted anew the thunderbolts of the land of Sodom. For it produced a *genea* far more godless than the victims of those visitations, seeing that these men's frenzy involved the whole people in their ruin".

19 Cf. the stress on the punishments of the Flood and in the desert in CD 2:14 ff.

20 See Jack P. Lewis, *A Study of the Interpretation of Noah and the Flood in Jewish and Christian Literature*, 1968, passim.

21 Wis 10:3 f.; cf.*Tg. Neof.* Gen 4:24.

view is taken in e.g. *T. Napth.* 3:5.[23]

Regardless of whether evil before the Flood is traced to Cain and his descendants or is blamed on 'the sons of God' and their influence, or possibly traced to yet another source, there is agreement that it was overwhelming. It is described as selfishness and disobedience to God (CD 2:17-21), as fornication, uncleanness and iniquity (*Jub.* 7:20, 21), as licentiousness and whoredom, injustice, hardness of heart, robbery etc.[24] Corruption reigned, and, according to some rabbis, it extended to both the animals and the earth.[25]

When דור המבול is spoken about, it is then the spiritual corruption and the accompanying punishment that are primary and decisive. That is the focus of interest.

דור המבול does thus not simply refer just to all those who lived at the time of the Flood. The term applies to those who were participants in the pervading corruption and therefore were struck by God's punishment. The *dor* and the punishment belong together. In *Tg. Neof.* the judgement is formulated thus: "In truth, the judgement of the *dara'* of the Flood is sealed (decided) before (me), to have it destroyed and blotted out from the midst of the world"[26]. The *dor* of the Flood was wiped out *in its entirety*. This is specific for them according to the ancient Jewish view. "Not a remnant of them was left".[27] This concept is mirrored in an interesting way in the following formulation in *b. Nid.* 61a (in connection with Gen 14:13: "But a fugitive came and told Abram"...): "R. Jochanan (d. 279) explained: This refers to Og who escaped the *dor* of the Flood (שפלט מדור המבול)".[28] It does not say that he did not perish in the Flood, or something similar to it, but that he escaped דור המבול. In Jewish thought, the *dor* of the Flood in its totality was so intimately connected to its punishment, that rescue from disaster in the Flood could be expressed in this way.

The description of Noah and his delivery is significant in this context. After all, Noah lived among the people of the *dor* of the Flood. But God found him righteous.[29] There could be differing opinions among

---

[22] Cf. R. Rubinkiewicz, *Die Eschatologie von Henoch 9-11 und das Neue Testament*, 1984, 126.

[23] "The watchers also changed the order of their nature, whom the Lord cursed at the Flood, on whose account he made the earth without inhabitants and fruitless."

[24] For rabbinical references see J.P. Lewis, *op. cit.* 127 f.

[25] J.P. Lewis *op. cit.*, 128. See also Str-B I, 961-964.

[26] *Tg. Neof.* Gen 6:3. Cf. *Lev. Rab.* 13:9 (33b).

[27] *Gen. Rab.* 38:6 (77b); cf. Gen 6:13,17; 7:4,21; *Jub.* 5:20.

[28] Cf. *b. Zeb.* 113b. A lively description of Og's salvation is given in *Pirqe R.El.* 23 (53b).

the rabbis as to whether Noah was righteous in an absolute sense or only in comparison with his unrighteous contemporaries.[29] Regardless of that, it was clear that he had a unique position compared to others in his surroundings. There was a different spirit in him.[31] And we now find that Noah is not regarded as appertaining to the *dor* of the Flood in spite of the fact that he lived with those who were struck by the Flood. He is seen as a surviving remant of humanity[32] but not of 'the *dor* of the Flood'. It can be said about him that he appeared as a herald in דור המבול[33] , but he is not considered to belong to that *dor*. He was segregated from it (*Num. Rab.* 14:12 [62a]), and there is a definite distinction made between Noah and the *dor* of the Flood.

This distinction can be seen in the way that certain passages in the Scriptures are applied to the *dor* of the Flood and others to Noah. There is an example in *Gen. Rab.* 30:1 (62a):

"'When the whirlwind passeth, the wicked is no more' (Prov 10:25a) - this refers to the *dor* of the Flood; 'but the righteous is an everlasting foundation' (Prov 10:25b) - this refers to Noah, as it is written, 'These are the generations of Noah: Noah was a righteous man' (Gen 6:9). 'The wicked are overthrown, and are not' (Prov 12:7a) - this refers to the *dor* of the Flood; 'but the house of the righteous shall stand' (ib. 7b) - this refers to Noah: 'These are the generations of Noah' (ib.). 'The house of the wicked shall be overthrown ' (Prov 14:11a) - this refers to the *dor* of the Flood; 'but the tent of the upright shall flourish' (ib. 11b) - this refers to Noah: 'These are the generations of Noah' (ib.).[34]

The rabbis also apply other scriptural passages to the *dor* of the Flood on the one hand and Noah on the other in a similar way.[35]

The contrast between Noah and the *dor* of the Flood is also expressed in the reference to '*Noah's* דור' as something separate from 'the דור of

---

[29] Noah's righteousness is a common topic; see e.g. Ezek 14:14,20; Sir. 44:17; *1 Enoch* 67:1; 81:1ff. *Jub.*10:17. Further J.C. VanderKam, "The Righteousness of Noah", *Ideal Figures in Ancient Judaism* (ed. Collins and Nickelsburg), 1980, 13-32; O. Christoffersson, *The Earnest Expectation of the Creature*, 1990, 73.

[30] See below p.57. - A certain tendency to 'reduce' the righteousness of Noah can be noticed in the rabbis; cf. Ch. Kaplan, "The Flood in the Book of Enoch and Rabbinics", *The Journal of the Society of Oriental Research* 15, 1931, 24; J. P. Lewis, *op. cit.*, 133.

[31] Cf below p. 107.

[32] Cf. Sir 44:17; *1 Enoch* 10:3; 65:12; 83:8; 106:16-18; *Lev. Rab.* 5:1 (8a). Cf. J. Daniélou, *Sacramentum futuri*, 1950, 60 f.

[33] E.g. *Gen. Rab.* 30:7 (62b).

[34] The passage is based on Gen 6:9 and illustrates, with references to the Scriptures, the fact that Noah, in contrast to the *dor* of the Flood, survived and was blessed with descendants. – Translation according to H. Freedman, Soncino Press ed.

[35] E.g. Ps 1:6 in *Midr. Ps.* 1 § 12 (6b).

the Flood'[36]. This strongly emphasizes that it is religious and moral character and the accompanying punishment which is the decisive and bearing factor in reference to דור המבול – NB the phrase 'the *dor* of *the Flood*' itself.

The *dor* of the Flood is simply the ungodly and sinful people before 'the first end of the world', who were struck down by God's annihilating punishment, those 'who corrupted their way and their counsel before the Flood' (*Jub.* 5:19).

The spiritual decay extended back in time from the Flood. Even if, as noted above, it can be traced back to Cain and his murder of Abel in early Jewish literature, it is usually traced back to the 'sons of God' and their actions according to Gen 6:2 f. These are said to have come to the earth in the days of Jared (*Jub* 4:15; *1 Enoch* 106:13 f.), i.e. in the fourth generation before Noah (Gen 5:18-29; *Jub.* 4:16-28). This, however, does not create a problem in the use of the term דור המבול in that context. The decision of God in Gen 6:3, based on the actions of the 'sons of God' with the daughters of men, can be interpreted by the rabbis as giving the *dor* of the Flood an extension of time of 120 years to repent.[37] It can be said that Enoch has been taken away 'from the sons of the *dor* of the Flood' (מן בני דור המבול)[38], etc. In the expression דור המבול itself there is no limitation of its extension backwards in time. It is inner characteristics, spiritual character and its accompanying punishment that are in focus.

The same features that are characteristic of the *dor* of the Flood are also characteristic of the *dor* of the Wilderness, דור המדבר. The latter is referred to several times in the Old Testament as an evil דור. It is called 'this wicked *dor*' (Deut 1:35), 'a perverse and crooked *dor*' (Deut 32:5), 'a mutinous *dor*' (Deut 32:20). Referring to them, it says in Ps 95:10 that God was indignant בדור, 'with that *dor*'. They were struck down by God's judgement: "all the *dor* (כל הדור) that had done evil in the eyes of IHWH" must die in the desert (Num 32:13). In post-biblical Jewish, especially rabbinic literature, the '*dor* of the Wilderness' is often mentioned. With their opposition to God and Moses, with their lack of faith which led to the severe punishment by God, they are

---

[36] E.g. *3 Enoch* 45:3: "I saw ... Noah and his *dor*, their doings and their thoughts, and the *dor* of the Flood, their doings and their thoughts".

[37] *Tg. Onq.*Gen. 6:3 says: "The Lord said, 'This evil *dara*' (דרא בישא הדין) shall not endure before me forever, because they are flesh and their works are evil. An extension of time will I give them, 120 years, if they may repent'". Likewise *Tg. Neof.* ad loc. Cf. *Mek.* Ex 15:6.

[38] *3 Enoch* 7:1; cf. 4:3. Cf. E. Sjöberg, *Der Menschensohn im äthiopischen Henochbuch*, 1946, 182 f.

referred to as a warning example.

It is true that דור המדבר[39] existed for a limited period of time, but that is not where the stress lies.The aspect is the same in this case as in the case of דור המבול. Here too it is a question of the character of the *dor* in their relation to God. It is their faithless and mutinous behaviour towards the Lord and his instrument (Moses) at the exodus and the following punishment that are at the centre of interest.

In spite of God's mighty intervention for their salvation the people of the first exodus did not believe in him. They challenged him and Moses.[40] Time after time they 'tempted' him.[41] They demanded that the Lord should show them some striking proof that he was with his people as their saviour and helper. The basic issue of the temptation is exposed in Ex 17:7: "Is the Lord in our midst or not?" At last God's judgement fell on them. It happened after the report from the wicked spies, which led to the rebellious reactions of the people to God's acts of salvation worked through Moses (Num 13-14).[42] They were sentenced to be lost in the desert (Num 32:13). It is their lack of faith in their dismissal of God's intervention for their delivery that characterized דור המדבר.

However, here too there were people who were not in spiritual affinity with the *dor*. Among them were Caleb and Joshua (Num 14:24–30; 26:65; 32:12; Deut 1:35-38).[43] They lived at the time of דור המדבר, but they were not of the same spirit as the *dor* and were therefore not struck by their judgement.

The situation of Moses arouses special interest in this context. He was refused permission to enter the Promised Land (Num 20:12). Does that mean that he is counted as one of the *dor* of the Wilderness in post-biblical writings? This is not the case. It is clearly marked that he is on another level. This can be exemplified by a passage in *Tanch.* חקת 32 (61, a,b; ed. Buber), where Moses says to the Lord[44]: "Behold, you

---

[39] As for the expression cf. the דור terminology in Num 32:13; Deut 32:5,20; Ps 95:10.

[40] See further E. Lövestam, *Spiritus blasphemia*, 1968, 17-34.

[41] Ex 17:2 ff.; Num 14:22; Ps 78:17 ff.; 95:9; 106:14 ff. etc.

[42] As for God's judgement in Kadesh according to the Old Testament and in early Jewish literature cf. O. Hofius, *Katapausis*, 1970, 118-127.

[43] Sometimes in this context reference is also made to others, such as Eleazar the priest (Num 34:17; Jos 14:1) and the whole tribe of Levi (cf. Ex 32:26). In *Midr. Ps.* 1 § 14 (7a,b) it is said for example, that the tribe of Levi did not walk in the counsel of the *dor* of the Wilderness (בעצת דור המדבר). Therefore the entire tribe entered the land of Israel, except Moses, Aaron and Miriam (the latter is traced to R. Joshua ben Levi, c. 250). Otherwise the judgement only applied to Israelites from twenty years old and upward (Num 14:29).

have decreed that I shall die in the wilderness with this evil *dor* (עם הדור הרע הזה)... And now, future generations will say that I was like them. Let the reason why I have been punished be recorded about me".[45] In spite of the fact that both Moses and the *dor* of the Wilderness were refused entry into the Promised Land, the differentiation between them is made clear. This marks where the emphasis lies in relation to דור המדבר.

This is also illustrated in several other ways. Among other things, a rabbinic comment on the changing of Joshua's name from Hoshea to Joshua (יְהוֹשֻעַ, LXX: Ἰησοῦς; Num 13:16) is illustrative in this connection. The question is posed as to what grounds Moses had for making the change, and the answer is, "When Moses saw that they (i.e. the spies) were very wicked he said to him (viz. Hoshea/Joshua): 'May God save you from this evil *dor* (יהוה יושיעך מן הדור הרע הזה)'".[46] It is assumed that Joshua *could* be saved from דור המדבר, as the stress in this concept is on spiritual character with its disastrous consequences. And Joshua *must* be saved from דור המדבר, if he was to escape the impending judgement, for the *dor* of the Wilderness were to die in the desert.

When in early Jewish literature דור המדבר, דור המבול and corresponding collectives are referred to, it is not days and years that are important. It is the character of the *dorot* and their relationship with God. This is apparent not only in the above-mentioned traits. It is also emphasized by the fact that the *dorot* in question are treated as homogeneous units eschatalogically. What will their fate be in the eschatological future? This question was discussed by rabbis in the 1st century AD. In *m. Sanh.* 10:3 it is stated: "The *dor* of the Flood have no portion in the future world, nor will they stand at the (last) judgement... The *dor* of the Wilderness have no share in the future world and will not stand at the (last) judgment..." According to another milder view the last-mentioned *dor* do have a future.[47] In that context an association is sometimes made to the fate of Moses. For the sake of him who died and was buried in the desert with 'the *dor*', it will be saved. It will be raised from the dead and, led by Moses, finally enter into the Promised Land, in accordance with the interpretation and application of Deut 33:21 in the midrash.[48]

---

[44] In connection with the words of judgement over Moses and Aron in Num 20:12.

[45] Par. *Num. Rab.*19:12 (80a) et al.

[46] *Tanch.* שלח 9 (33a; ed. Buber); par. *Num.Rab.*16:9 (69a).

[47] In *m. Sanh.* 10:3 the stricter attitude to the *dor* of the Wilderness is attributed to R. Akiba (d. c. 135 AD) and the milder to R. Eliezer (c. 90 AD). For more on the rabbinical discussions on this matter see e.g. O. Hofius, *Katapausis*, 1970, 44.

[48] See J. Jeremias, Μωυσῆς, *TWNT* 4, 858, 861.

דור המבול and דור המדבר were thus well profiled concepts – even from the eschatological point of view – in the ancient Jewish world of ideas.

2. The ἡ γενεὰ αὕτη Conception in the New Testament and its Roots in early Judaism. An introductory Survey

A general view of the ἡ γενεὰ αὕτη texts in the New Testament shows a manifest affinity with the *dor/genea* conceptions stated above. The following characteristics can be noticed:

1. The wording ἡ γενεὰ αὕτη, with the regularly post-placed αὕτη, goes back to a Semitic original (הַדּוֹר הַזֶּה, e.g. Gen 7:1), and the often accompanying adjectives usually relate back to Old Testament sayings concerning the *dor* of the Wilderness.[49]

2. In their contexts in the New Testament, the ἡ γενεὰ αὕτη passages bring to the fore not only one of the above-mentioned *dorot/geneai*, but at least two, the *dor* of the Wilderness and that of the Flood (Lk 17:25 ff.; Mt 24:34 ff.), a fact which emphasizes their structural affinity with the conception in question.

3. In common with the *dor* of the Flood and the *dor* of the Wilderness, ἡ γενεὰ αὕτη in the New Testament has generally an obvious pejorative tone, formulated in the accompanying adjectives and/or indicated by the context (Mk 8:12; Lk 17:25).

4. Like the above-mentioned *dorot*, ἡ γενεὰ αὕτη is also on its way towards divine judgement (e.g. Mt 12:41 f. par. Lk 11:30-32; Mt 23:36 par. Lk 11:50 f.).

5. Even in the New Testament the *dor/genea* is regarded as a homogeneous unit eschatologically: At the last judgement the men of Nineveh and the Queen of the South will ensure the condemnation of ἡ γενεὰ αὕτη (Mt 12:41 f. par. Lk 11:30-32).

6. Just as Noah was a contemporary of the *dor* of the Flood and yet did not belong to it and men like Moses, Caleb and Joshua were contemporaries of the *dor* of the Wilderness without belonging to it, it is assumed in the New Testament that there are contemporaries (Jesus, of course, and others) who do not belong to 'this *genea*'. This emphasizes the decisive and demarcating stress on the spiritual character in the ἡ γενεὰ αὕτη concept. It can from this point of view be compared with such a conception as ὁ αἰὼν οὗτος.

7. It is also true in the New Testament that the people of the *genea* referred to must repent in order to escape judgment and be saved. Here,

---

[49] See above p. 8.

as in early Jewish texts, the appeal to them to convert can be related to the *genea* in its entirety (e.g. Mt 12:41 par. Lk 11:32) as well as to the individual people in relation to ἡ γενεὰ αὕτη with its ungodly character (e.g. Acts 2:40).

In light of these facts, there can be no doubt that ἡ γενεὰ αὕτη in the New Testament has as its background the above stated conceptions in ancient Judaism and should be seen from this point of view. It is true that the γενεά in question is not identified there by formulations such as 'the *dor* of the Flood' and 'the *dor* of the Wilderness' but by pointing it out as ἡ γενεὰ αὕτη. This, however, does not imply any real difference. When the *dorot* of the Flood and the Wilderness are assumed to be contemporary with the speaker or reader – as in the case with 'this *genea*' on the lips of Jesus – they are also mentioned in the same way, e.g. Gen 7:1: בדור הזה (LXX: ἐν τῇ γενεᾷ ταύτῃ, i.e. the *dor* of the Flood), Deut 1:35: הדור הרע הזה (the *dor* of the Wilderness), *Tg. Onq.* Gen 6:3: דרא בישא הדין (the *dor* of the Flood), *Tanch.* חקת 32 (61a; ed. Buber): הדור הרע הזה (the *dor* of the Wilderness), *Tanch.* שלח 9 (33a; ed. Buber): הדור הרע הזה (the *dor* of the Wilderness), etc.[50]

What is it then that gives ἡ γενεὰ αὕτη its special quality of an evil and faithless *genea*? A survey of the relevant material shows that the expression is almost always found in contexts where people's negative attitude to Jesus, the Son of Man, is in focus: in the parable of the children in the market-place (Mt 11:16 ff. par. Lk 7:31 ff.), in the texts of the demand for a sign (Mk 8:11 ff.; Mt 16:1 ff.; 12:39 ff. par. Lk 11:16,29 ff.), in the prophesies that the Son of Man must endure much suffering and be repudiated by 'this *genea*' (Lk 17:25) and that anyone who is ashamed of him and his word in 'this faithless and sinful *genea*' shall be rejected at the judgement (Mk 8:38), and in Peter's Pentecost appeal to the people to let themselves be saved from 'this crooked *genea*' which put Jesus on the cross (Acts 2:40), etc. It is thus the faithless, rejecting attitude of people to God's act of salvation in Jesus, the Son of Man, which causes the negative connotations of ἡ γενεὰ αὕτη. This salvation-historical orientation is further accentuated by the fact that the expression can also include a reference to the forerunner (Mt 11:16 ff. par. Lk 7:31 ff.) as well as to the messengers sent out by Jesus (Mt 23:34 ff. par. Lk 11:49 ff.).

Furthermore, the allusions to the *dor* of the Wilderness and the *dor* of the Flood place ἡ γενεὰ αὕτη in a typological perspective.[51]

---

[50] Cf. the phrase 'this (evil) generation' in *Jub.* 23:15,16.

[51] As for the typology aspect in the New Testament see e.g. D.L. Baker, "Typology and the Christian Use of the Old Testament", *SJT* 29, 1976, 137–157; E.E. Ellis,.

The typology of *the Flood* (the first end of the world)–*t h e eschatological judgement* (the second end of the world) is well documented in early Jewish literature as well as in the New Testament.[52] The same applies to the typology of *the first exodus–the second exodus.*[53]

The Old Testament in Early Christianity, 1991, 105–109.

[52] See e.g. Bo Reicke, *The Disobedient Spirits and Christian Baptism*, 1946, 70 ff.; J. Daniélou, *Sacramentum futuri*, 1950, 55 ff.; J.P. Lewis, *A Study of the Interpretation of Noah and the Flood in Jewish and Christian Literature,* 1968; O. Christoffersson, *The Earnest Expectation of the Creature. The Flood-Tradition as Matrix of Romans 8:18–27*, 1990, passim.

[53] See among others W. Wiebe, *Die Wüstenzeit als Typus der messianischen Heilszeit*, 1939 (typed); J. Daniélou, *op. cit.*, 131-200; R.E. Nixon, *The Exodus in the New Testament*, 1963; U. W. Mauser, *Christ in the Wilderness* , 1963; H. Ulfgard, *Feast and Future*, 1989, 35–41 and passim. – For the desert motif in the Dead Sea Scrolls see e.g. S. Talmon, "The 'Desert Motif' in the Bible and in Qumran Literature", *Biblical Motifs* (ed. A. Altmann), 1966, 31–63; L.H. Schiffman, *The Eschatological Community of the Dead Sea Scrolls*, 1989, passim.

3. The synoptic Texts of the Demand for a Sign

There is a context in the New Testament where the phrase ἡ γενεὰ αὕτη appears with striking consistency. It is in connection with the demand for a sign in the synoptic Gospels (Mk 8:11-13 par. Mt 16:1-4; Lk 11:16, 29-32 par. Mt 12:38-42).

All the Synoptics describe how people ask Jesus to show them a sign (from heaven). The question occurs in a short version (Mk 8:11-13 and Mt 16:1-4) and a long one (Lk 11:16, 29-32 and Mt 12:38-42). Some aspects of the description of the scene also vary. Among them is the identity of the questioners[54] and the reference to the sign of Jonah.[55] The texts are, however, all in agreement in this respect, that they bring to the fore the conception of 'this *genea*'. The formulation itself varies somewhat. While Mk uses the phrase ἡ γενεὰ αὕτη (8:12), in the parallel passage Mt has γενεὰ πονηρὰ καὶ μοιχαλίς (16:4). The same expression is also to be found in Mt 12:39, while a few verses later it says ἡ γενεὰ αὕτη (12:41-42) and ἡ γενεὰ αὕτη ἡ πονηρά (v. 45) respectively. In Lk it says ἡ γενεὰ αὕτη γενεὰ πονηρά ἐστιν (11:29), after which the phrase ἡ γενεὰ αὕτη reappears in vs. 31 and 32.

That 'this *genea*' terminology is repeatedly present in these texts can hardly be a coincidence. The circumstances make them particularly interesting in the context here.

In three of the four texts it is said that they are about a sign 'from heaven' (Mk 8:11; Mt 16:1; Lk 11:16). This does not necessarily mean a deed or an intervention of a cosmic-apocalyptic nature.[56] The demand made on Jesus implies a demand for divine authorization. He is asked for a sign, which will show without any doubt that God is with him, that he has been sent by God and acts through the power of God.[57] Cf. the second/third temptation in Mt 4:5-7 / Lk 4:9-12.

---

[54] Mk names the Pharisees (8:11), while the parallel passage in Mt names the Pharisees and Sadducees (16:1). In Mt 12:38 the doctors of the law and the Pharisees are mentioned, while Lk in the same context expresses himself more vaguely: 'Others' (of the people; 11:16). Cf. S. van Tilborg, *The Jewish Leaders in Matthew*, 1972, 30.

[55] See below.

[56] Cf. O. Linton, "The Demand for a Sign from Heaven", *ST* 19, 1965, 112-129.

[57] Cf. the meaning of ἐξ οὐρανοῦ in Mk 11:30. In the ancient Jewish environment 'heaven' could be used as a designation for God (see e.g. G. Dalman, *Die Worte Jesu*, 2nd ed. 1930, 178 ff.).

The demand for a sign belongs primarily in the conceptual world which is related to the *prophet* and his claims.[58] It is possible that expectations of the awaited prophet like Moses are involved (Deut 18:15,18) - note Deut 34:10 f.: there has not arisen a prophet like Moses since in Israel "for all the signs and the wonders which the Lord sent him to do"....[59] Regardless of this, on closer analysis it is apparent that it is the concept of the *dor* of the Wilderness and the ideas connected to it that are primarily in the background - with the repeated adjective πονηρός it is in the first place the formulation in Dt 1:35 which is recognizable in the phrase (הַדּוֹר הָרָע הַזֶּה; cf. above p. 8).[60]

It is an integral part of the picture of the liberation from Egypt and the wandering in the wilderness that the Israel which challenged Moses (and thus God) and therefore was punished by the Lord, had earlier witnessed his extraordinary actions to help and save them.[61] That is an aspect which is underlined in the Old Testament presentations. The desert wanderers are described as "the men who have seen my glory and my signs which I wrought in Egypt and in the wilderness" but who nevertheless rebelled (Num 14:22). "Despite his wonders they did not believe" (Ps 78:32). They did not keep in mind "how he set his signs in Egypt, his portents in the land of Zoan" (Ps 78:43; cf. vs. 12 ff.). They "forgot his works" (Ps 106:13), "they forgot God their deliverer, who had done great deeds in Egypt, marvels in the land of Ham, terrible things at the Red Sea" (v. 21 f.), etc.[62] In spite of all the mighty deeds and miracles they had seen they did not rely on God. Instead they repeatedly made their own demands on him (Ex 17:2 ff.; Num 11:4 ff.; Ps 78:17 ff.; 106:14 etc.).[63]

---

[58] Cf. F. Hahn, *Christologische Hoheitstitel*, 2nd ed. 1964, 390 f.; K.H. Rengstorf, σημεῖον κτλ., *TWNT* 7, 1964, 234; J. Jeremias, *Neutestamentliche Theologie* I, 1971, 82.

[59] Ideas about the eschatological prophet like Moses and of the coming Messiah were not infrequently associated and affected each other; cf. F. Hahn, *op. cit.,* 369 ff.; R. Leivestad, *Hvem ville Jesus være?*, 1982, 64 f.

[60] References have also been made to Ps 95 [94]:10 and/or Deut 32:5; cf. A.H. M'Neile, *The Gospel according to St. Matthew*, 1915 (1965), 157; M.-J. Lagrange, *Evangile selon Saint Marc*, 1947, 207; J. Guillet, "Cette génération infidèle et dévoyée", *RSR* 35, 1948, 278 f.; V. Taylor, *The Gospel according to St. Mark,* 1957, 362; R. Pesch, *Das Markusevangelium* I, 1976, 408.

[61] On the question of the miracles and the exodus cf. J. Bowman, *The Gospel of Mark. The New Christian Jewish Passover Haggadah,* 1965, 77–89; F.Stolz, "Zeichen und Wunder. Die prophetische Legitimation und ihre Geschichte", *ZThK* 69, 1972, 125-144.

[62] Cf. Pseudo-Philo, *Liber Antiqitatum Biblicarum* 15:5 f.

[63] Cf. K.H. Regnstorf, γογγύζω κτλ., *TWNT* 1, 730.

These demands were not only made in order to get help in critical situations. They were also made in an attempt to achieve an indisputable sign that God lay behind the enterprise. The suffering in the desert made the people turn against Moses with the question: "Why have you brought us out of Egypt?" (Ex 17:3). Could they be sure that it was God's directions they were following? "Is the Lord in our midst or not?" (v. 7). And could the Lord help them? "Can God spread a table in the wilderness? ... Can he give bread, can he provide meat for his people?" (Ps 78:19 f.). They wanted proof of God's power and his care for them if they were to trust him (and Moses). This aspect is marked in some rabbinical comments on the main passage Ex 17:7, e.g. in *Mek. Ex.* in loc.: "R. Joshua (c. 90 AD) says: The Israelites said: If he is master over all the works as he is master over us we will serve him, but if he is not, we will not serve him. R. Eliezer (c. 90 AD) says: They said: If he supplies all our needs we will serve him, but if he does not, we will not serve him."[64]

When the people demanded God's intervention, this is classified in the texts as belonging to the category of 'putting to the test'. It is mainly the term נסה (LXX: /ἐκ/πειράζειν) which is used. In Num 14:22 the Lord declares: "Ten times have they put me to the proof and not obeyed my voice". The Talmud identifies the ten proofs in the following way: twice at the Red Sea, twice in the case of the manna, twice in the case of the quails, twice when they lacked water (at Marah and at Rephidim), once by worshipping the golden calf and once by accepting the evil report of the spies.[65] The central role of the concept of testing in this context is made clear by the name מַסָּה (LXX: Πειρασμός)[66] of the place where Israel had disputed with the Lord and put him to the test according to Ex 17:1-7.[67] Those who put the Lord to the proof attacked his godly sovereignty by stating their own terms and demands, instead of believing in him and his messenger and being open for his powerful deeds and trusting his works of salvation.[68] That was what the

---

[64] In *Pesiq.Rab Kah.* 28a R. Eliezer's pronouncement - here traced to R. Nehemiah (c. 150 AD) - is combined with a simile about a king in the following way: "They said: If he supplies us food like a king, who resides in a provence and that provence then lacks nothing, will we serve him, but if not, we will be rebellious against him". Cf. W. Bacher, *Die Agada der Tannaiten* 1, 2nd ed. 1903, 210; II, 1890, 253, where parallel passages are given.

[65] *b. Arak.*15ab; cf. *m. 'Abot* 5:7; *'Abot R. Nat.*9; *Midr. Ps*. 95 § 3 (210b-211a).

[66] Together with מְרִיבָה, 'Dispute'; Ex 17:7.

[67] See also Ex 17:2; Deut 6:16; Ps 78:18,41; 95:8; 106:14.

[68] On the theme of the temptation during the wandering in the desert cf. H. Seesemann, πεῖρα κτλ., *TWNT* 6, 27; B. Gerhardsson, *The Testing of God's Son*, 1966,

Israel of the exodus did. And in this way they disclosed their doubt and their lack of faith.

In rabbinic writings we can even find the opinion that the people in the desert were not honest in their demands. The real purpose was in fact to find an excuse to free themselves from God.[69]

Within the framework of the exodus typology in the New Testament, connections are sometimes also made to that fact that the people of the first exodus reacted to God's acts of salvation with doubt and disbelief and rebellious behaviour. So, e.g. when Jesus in the story of the temptation answers the Tempter with an allusion to Deut 6:16 (with its reference to what happened at Massah): "You shall not put the Lord your God to the test" (Mt 4:7 par. Lk 4:12). Or when Paul uses the story of the behaviour of those wandering in the wilderness for the purpose of giving a warning in 1 Cor 10:1-11 and among other things states: "We must not put the Lord (v.1. Christ) to the test, as some of them did" (v.9). Or when those addressed in Heb 3:7-4:11 are exorted not to behave like Israel during the wandering in the desert, as they then would not be allowed to come into God's eschatological rest - with Ps 95:7b-11 as the scriptural reference.[70] The theme was certainly topical.

In this 'dor of the Wilderness' perspective the gospel texts of the demand for a sign from heaven acquire their significant meaning.

According to all the Synoptics, this demand comes after Jesus has carried out several of his mighty works (Mk 1:23 ff.; 2:1 ff.; Mt 8-9; 12:22 ff; Lk 4:33 ff.; 5:12 ff. etc.). Just as God had acted at the time of the first exodus with signs and miracles "in Egypt and in the desert" to save the people (Num 14:22 et al.), so has he caused spectacular events to take place through Jesus at the time of the second exodus. But the people are not satisfied by these deeds. They do not accept them as an expression of the Lord's acts of salvation. They want tangible and unequivocal proof that God is present and acting in and through him. It is the question from the time of the wandering in the wilderness that returns here: "Is the Lord in our midst or not?" (Ex 17:7). They want this guaranteed if they are to put their faith in Jesus.

Here the aspect of proof in the Gospels comes into focus in a significant way. All the Synoptics emphasize that Pharisees and others made their demand on Jesus for a sign in order to test him (πειράζοντες /αὐτόν/; Mk 8:11; Mt 16:1; Lk 11:16). True, it would

28 ff.

[69] Sipre Num. § 95 (26a; R. Shimeon b. Jochai, c. 150); par. § 86 (23b); cf. § 85 (23a). For par. t. Sota 6:7 and Sipre Deut. § 31 see K.G. Kuhn, Der tannaitische Midrasch Sifre zu Numeri, 1959, 253 n. 1.

[70] More on this below in chap. 10b.

appear to be legitimate in ancient Israel to put to a test anyone making claims to be sent by God in a special sense. They had to protect themselves and others from false prophets and fraudulent leaders. In this case, however, the term πειράζειν has undoubtedly the same meaning as in the exodus texts of the Old Testament, when the challenges to God (Moses) during the desert-wandering are regarded there as a 'putting to the test'. And as the wanderers in the wilderness, in spite of all the powerful acts they have witnessed, are not satisfied but put the Lord (Moses) to the proof, it is a symptom of lack of faith. The circumstances are the same when the people ask for a sign from Jesus, πειράζοντες αὐτόν. Their reaction is due to lack of faith. Nor do the texts in question give any reasons for excluding this aspect, which has been seen to be expressed by some rabbis, namely, that the people in the desert asked for a special act of God (Moses) as a means of finding an excuse not to listen to him or to obey him.

Against that background, the consistent occurrence of the דור/γενεά-terminology in this context becomes important. In early Israel the concept of the 'dor of the Wilderness' was associated with the knowledge of the faithless reactions of the people at the time of the first exodus. When, in a similar way, the people now demand a sign as proof from Jesus and he in his answer speaks in a negative fashion of 'this genea' with a terminology which refers back to that of the desert wanderers, it recalls without doubt דור המדבר.[71] Those who have experienced his divine mission, listened to his preaching and witnessed his mighty deeds - 'by the Spirit (finger) of God' (Mt 12:28; Lk 11:20) - but met him with doubt and contradiction, have a typological 'forerunner' in the faithless people of the first exodus.

That, in fact, discloses the current situation in two ways. It means an indication of the fact that Jesus was sent as 'the second Redeemer', preceded by the first one, Moses. And it reveals the plight of those who do not believe in him but come with their demand for a sign. Like the dor of the Wilderness they are on a path that leads to a radical judgement – here in an eschatalogical perspective (Mt 12:41 f. par. Lk 11:31 f.).

The comment in Mk 8:13 par. Mt 16:4 that Jesus leaves those who ask for a sign after he has given a dismissive answer, has probably also a function in this connection. In the Song of Moses in Deut 32[72] the

---

[71] Deut 1:35: הדור הרע הזה; cf. the examples from *Tanchuma* on p. 19.

[72] The origin and character of the song of Moses in itself will not be discussed here. What is important in this context is the interpretation and application of the sayings of the Scriptures in the ancient Jewish and early Christian time.

Lord says in v. 20 - in connection with the concept of the *dor* of the Wilderness - that he will hide his face from them and see what their end will be. In early Jewish texts this is sometimes expressed by saying that he will remove his Shekinah, his divine Presence.[73] Seen in this light, the emphasis on Jesus – sent by God and working in the power of God (the Spirit) - leaving those who ask for a sign, acquires a special dimension. It expresses in the form of an action the impending judgement on a wicked and adulterous *genea*.

In Mk 8:12 the negative answer of Jesus to the demand for a sign is formulated without exception as follows: "No sign shall be given to this *genea*". The parallel passage in Mt 16:4 refers to 'the sign of Jonah': "No sign shall be given to it except the sign of Jonah". The same is the case in Mt 12:39 f. par. Lk 11:29 f. There it is formulated in the same way as Mt 16:4, but in both the two last-named passages it is expressed more fully. Both in Mt 12 and par. Lk 11 the double comparison of the Ninevites and the Queen of the South follow but in a different order (Mt 12:41 f. and Lk 11:31 f.).[74]

The statement about 'the sign of Jonah'[75] is the only context in the New Testament where the prophet Jonah is mentioned.[76] It is self-evident that the saying in some way or other relates to what is said in the book of Jonah in the Old Testament: about the command of the Lord

---

[73] See further below p. 54 f.

[74] For the tradition-historical aspects cf. R. Edwards, *The Sign of Jonah*, 1971; J. Fitzmyer, *The Gospel of Luke X-XXIV*, 1985, 930-932; U. Luz, *Das Evangelium nach Matthäus* II, 1990, 273-275 (with ref.).

[75] Among the extensive literature on the sign of Jonah can be mentioned J. Jeremias, Ἰωνᾶς, *TWNT* 3, 410-413; P. Seidelin, "Das Jonaszeichen", *ST* 5, 1951, 119-131; A. Vögtle, "Der Spruch vom Jonaszeichen" (1953) in id., *Das Evangelium und die Evangelien*, 1971, 103-136; O. Glombitza, "Das Zeichen des Jona", *NTS* 8, 1962, 359-366; K.H. Rengstorf, σημεῖον κτλ., *TWNT* 7, 231 f.; Richard A. Edwards, *The Sign of Jonah in the Theology of the Evangelists and Q*, 1971; S. Schulz, *Q. Die Spruchquelle der Evangelisten*, 1972, 250-257; G. Schmitt, "Das Zeichen des Jona", *ZNW* 69, 1978, 123-129; J. Swetnam, "Some Signs of Jonah", *Bib* 68, 1987, 74-79; U. Luz, *op. cit.*, 275–280; W.D. Davies - D.C. Allison, *A Critical and Exegetical Commentary on the Gospel according to Saint Matthew* II, 1991, 351–353; H. Schürmann, *Das Lukasevangelium* II:1, 1994, 268–290; A. Vögtle, *Die 'Gretchenfrage' des Menschensohnproblems*, 1994, 148–163. – In *The Lives of the Prophets* (probably from the first cent. A.D.) it is said about Jonah: "He gave a portent (τέρας) concerning Jerusalem and the whole land, that whenever they should see a stone crying out piteously the end was at hand" (Jonah 8 /10/). It has, however, rightly been pointed out that it is very difficult to imagine that a crying stone can have had anything to do with Jesus' reference to the sign of Jonah (Davies-Allison, *op. cit.*, 355).

[76] For Jonah in early Jewish literature see e.g. Str-B 1, 642-649; P. Seidelin, "Das Jonazeichen", *ST* 5, 1951, 122–128.

to the prophet to go to Nineveh and denounce the city; about his unsuccessful attempt to escape this task by fleeing on a ship going to Tarshish; about the Ninevites believing God's word brought to them by Jonah and their departure from their wicked ways; about God's repentance of the evil which he had said he would bring upon them and his compassion for Nineveh. However, that does not give any direct answer to the question as to what is meant by 'the sign of Jonah'.

In Mt and Lk an interpretation or application of this 'sign' is given.[77] According to Mt 12:39 f. the Son of Man will be three days and three nights[78] in the heart of the earth as Jonah was three days and three nights in the sea-monster's belly. The latter clearly refers to Jon 2:1: "Jonah was in the belly of the fish three days and three nights". This statement is followed in Jon 2 by the prophet's hymn of prayer in vs. 3-10. With the help of mythical pictures of death, the precarious situation of the person praying is strongly expressed. But in the hymn the rescue is also stressed: "You brought my life up from the pit, O Lord my God" (v. 6). Seen from this contextual perspective[79] the rescue/resurrection must be regarded as being implied in the typology of Mt although it is not explicitly expressed in words.

It is manifest that Jonah's experiences are not the sort of sign of authority that was asked of Jesus. It does not refer to something that the prophet carried out to demonstrate his divine authorization. Both the incident of Jonah and the sea-monster and the death and resurrection of Jesus are integrated elements in their mission and task. In the former case it is something that is crucial to Jonah and his prophetic mission and in the latter it is a matter of the central element in the Messianic call and work of Jesus.

In the parallel text in Luke (Lk 11:16, 29 f.) we find this application: "For as Jonah became a sign to the men of Nineveh, so will the Son of Man be to 'this *genea*'" (v. 30). This interpretation is so general that it is difficult to grasp its meaning. Does it mean that Jonah became a sign to the Ninevites by coming as God's prophet from a far country and pronouncing judgement on their city? 'The sign of Jonah' would then in

---

[77] As regards which of the two sayings is the original, a large majority of scholars place Lk foremost for good reasons. At the same time it is now and then also stated that it cannot be assumed that Jesus spoke about the sign of Jonah only once and on one occasion .

[78] The reference to time is not of such an exact character that Mt sees any conflict between 'three days and three nights' and 'the third day' when Jesus rose from the dead (Mt 16:21; 17:23 etc.); see Mt 27:63 ("after three days") - 27:64 ("until the third day"); cf. U. Lutz, *op. cit.* II, 277 f.

[79] Cf. P. Seidelin, *op. cit.*, 122–124.

Lk refer to the Son of Man, coming from afar as a heaven-sent preacher of repentance.[80] Or does it refer to the arrival of the Son of Man at the *parousia,* where he appears as a judge?[81] Or is the *tertium comparationis* salvation from death, so that Jesus' resurrection is meant?[82] Regardless of the circumstances, 'the sign of Jonah' is clearly not related to any authorising deeds of the kind that people were thinking of when they addressed their demand for a sign to Jesus.

[80] In Jon 3:4 f. it is merely said that Jonah preached about the destruction of the town in forty days and that the people believed God and acted thereafter. In post-biblical Jewish literature the prophetic message is also stressed in this context. It is stated that never before had a prophet been sent to 'the nations of the world' (L. Ginzberg, *The Legends of the Jews* VI, 349 n. 27 with ref.), that only one prophet was sent to Nineveh "and she turned in penitence" (*Lam. Rab.* Proems 31 [8b]), etc. The legend says that Jonah's voice from the square at Nineveh could be heard at great distances; this is seen from the perspective that his message reached into every house in the town (for ref. see Str-B 1, 647). - Among the scholars who support the interpretation in question see e.g. J. Fitzmyer, *The Gospel according to Saint Luke X-XXIV,* 1985, 933; U. Luz, *Das Evangelium nach Matthäus* II, 1990, 275, 278 f. In the presupposed situation the preaching of Jesus is, however, an ongoing activity and a problem is then the future tense form: the Son of Man *will* be (ἔσται) a sign... Is that to be understood as a logical future? Fitzmyer finds the note of irony unmistakable here, "since the sign is already being given" (*op. cit.* 933, 936).

[81] See e.g. R. Bultmann, *Die Geschichte der synoptischen Tradition,* 7. Aufl. 1967, 124; D. Lührmann, *Die Redaktion der Logienquelle,* 1969, 40 f.; M. Reiser, *Die Gerichtspredigt Jesu,* 1990, 192 (with ref.). It does, however, not correspond completely to Jonah's deeds in Nineveh which meant that he prophecied future punishment in such a way that it led to the repentance of the Ninevites who were thus saved, not that he passed definite judgement; cf. below p. 29–31.

[82] A problem about this interpretation is that Jonah is said here to have become a sign to 'the men of Nineveh'. But Jonah's experience at sea is not mentioned as a kind of authorization for him in Nineveh either in the book of Jonah or in early Jewish literature. It has, however, been pointed out that in a Jewish legend the sailors who threw the prophet into the sea saw all the remarkable things that God did unto Jonah and due to this felt impelled to cast away everyone his god and convert to the Jewish faith. In that context God's actions with Jonah are also called 'signs' (מותא); *Pirqe R. El.* 10 (26b). Reference has also been made to the fact that in 3 Macc it seems to be assumed that Jonah's relatives were told of the prophet's rescue when it says, "When Jonah was pining away unpitied in the belly of the monster of the deep, you, Father, restored him uninjured to all his household" (3 Macc 6:8). See J. Jeremias, 'Ιωνᾶς, *TWNT* 3, 413 n. 26. Even if it is not documented that the prophet's experiences with the big fish in the sea and his remarkable rescue had any importance in his appearances at Nineveh, it can, of course, not be ruled out that the Ninevites are expected to have known about it and have been impressed by it. – For the view that the *tertium comparationis* is salvation from death and that it is thus Jesus' resurrection that is meant, see Jeremiah, *op. cit.,* 413; H. Schürmann, *op. cit.,* 270–285; A. Vögtle, *Die 'Gretchenfrage' des Menschensohnproblems,* 1994, 148–163. According to Vögtle the manifestation will occur at the *parousia:* ..."diese ungläubige Generation werde den MS [Menschensohn] bei der Parusie als wunderbar aus dem Tod Erretteten erfahren" (p. 157 f.).

In the shorter version of the matter of a sign in Mk 8:11-12 and Mt 16:1-4, there is only reference to 'the sign of Jonah' in the latter, here without any comments (v. 4). It is reasonable to assume that the phrase is intended to have the same meaning in this passage as in the same context four chapters earlier in the gospel.

When it is thus quite clear that 'the sign of Jonah' has a completely different character to the flamboyant manifestation demanded of Jesus as a sign of divine authorization, it means that it constitutes no real difference in relation to the other texts, that Jesus in Mk 8:12 refuses the demand in question without referring to this 'sign'.[83]

Jesus' answer is followed in Mt and Lk with a judgement on 'this *genea*'. This is given in the form of a double-word with references to the men of Nineveh/Jonah and to the Queen of the South/Solomon respectively and with a contrast between the Ninevites and the Queen on the one hand and on the other hand 'this *genea*' at judgement (Mt 12:41 f. / Lk 11:31 f.).[84]

If the phrase 'the sign of Jonah' brought to the fore the story of Jonah and the people of Nineveh, there is a connection made to it again here. It is then the *repentance* of the Ninevites that is emphasized. At the judgement they will 'condemn' 'this *genea*', "for they repented at the preaching of Jonah ...." (Mt 12:41 / Lk 11:32).

In the book of Jonah it is a central point that the Ninevites listened to the prophet and repented and made penance and therefore escaped punishment (Jon 3:5-10). It is something which people return to in post-biblical texts regarding the theme of *repentance*. Thus, for example in *m. Ta'an* 2:1, the men of Nineveh are given as an example in that respect. And in connection with the passage in Jer 18:8 about a nation that turns (שׁוב) from its evil, it is asked in *Ex. Rab.* 45:1 (74a): "Who is that nation?". The answer is: "The men of Nineveh", whereupon it is further discussed in connection with the book of Jonah up to the point where it is said in ch. 3:10 that God withdrew the expected punishment.[85]

It is of special interest in this context that the heathen inhabitants of Nineveh are sometimes contrasted with Israel in this respect by the

---

[83] Cf. J. Jeremias, *op. cit.*, 413; P. Seidelin, *op. cit.*, 131; D. Lührmann, *Die Redaktion der Logienquelle*, 1969, 41; W.D. Davies-D.C. Allison, *op. cit.*, 352; H. Schürmann, *op. cit.*, 272.

[84] The order between the above-mentioned references is different in Mt and Lk, and it is scarcely possible to say which is the primary. It is also difficult to judge with any certainty the connection between the double-word and the previous answer to the demand for a sign seen in a redaction-historical persepective. The parallel between Mt and Lk suggests, however, that it at least is pre-synoptic.

[85] For other rabbinic passages on the repentance of Nineveh see Str-B 1, 647 f.

rabbis. As in e.g. *Lam. Rab.* Proems 31 (8b): "One prophet I sent to Nineveh and she turned in penitence (בתשובה); but to Israel in Jerusalem I sent many prophets" - and the people did not hearken. There is particular reason here to emphasize the motive given for Jonah's attempt to escape God's task as it is mentioned in several places in the rabbis. In *Mek.* Ex 12:1 it is put as follows: "Jonah thought: I will go outside of the land, where the Shekinah does not reveal itself. For since the Gentiles are more inclined to repent (לתשובה), I might be causing Israel to be condemned (לחייב)".[86] The readiness of the Ninevites to listen to the prophet and repent could be a judgement on the unrepentent Israel. Jonah wished to avoid that, and it was therefore he tried to flee, it is said. At times the repentence of the Ninevites has been made to appear less significant by positing that it was in fact illusory and that the people of Nineveh soon returned to their sinful ways and received their punishment.[87]

In the above quoted text from *Mekilta* both the term תְּשׁוּבָה 'repentance' and חַיֵּב 'to prove to be in the wrong', 'to bring down condemnation' occur.[88] This is most interesting as this terminology (in the Greek form) can also be found in Jesus' contrasting of the Ninevites and 'this *genea*' in Mt 12:41 par. Lk 11:32: "Ninevites will arise at the judgement with 'this *genea*' and '*condemn*' (κατακρινοῦσιν) it; for they *repented* (μετενόησαν) at the preaching of Jonah, and behold, something greater than Jonah is here" - κατακρίνειν should be traced back to חייב.[89] The striking affinity of terminology and content in this case make it justifiable to ask if Jesus perhaps knew of the tradition in question and deliberately made reference to it.[90] Whatever the circumstances, we find in the words of Jesus the same line of thought as in early Jewish literature: the heathen Ninevites, through their obedience and repentance, become a judgement on the unrepentant people of God. In the gospel texts it is then 'this *genea*' on which judgement is passed.

The rooting of the Jonah/repentance of the Ninevites theme in ancient Judaism is further marked by the fact that it is even manifested

[86] Further references in Str-B 1, 643 f.

[87] L. Ginzberg, *The Legends of the Jews* IV, 1913, 252 f.; VI, 1928, 351; cf. Str-B 1, 647 f.

[88] See J. Jeremias in *TWNT* 3, 411 n. 16

[89] E.g. G. Dalman, *Die Worte Jesu* I, 1930, 51; Jeremias, ibid. (with ref.); see further below p. 36 n. 104.

[90] Cf. M. Reiser, *Die Gerichtspredigt Jesu*, 1990, 200: "Diese erstaunliche Übereinstimmung lässt vermuten, dass Jesus die angeführte Tradition kannte und möglicherweise sogar bewusst darauf anspielte".

lithurgically. In a Baraitha it is said about the readings on the Day of Atonement: "At *minchah* we read the section of forbidden marriages (i.e. Lev 18) and for *haftarah* the book of Jonah" (*b. Meg.* 31a). While we know very little about the selection of prophetic lessons for the various festivals in New Testament times, from this - as D. Daube puts it – "it is virtually certain that Jonah was, if not the prescribed, at least the usual reading for the afternoon of the Day of Atonement".[91]

It can be seen above that the synoptic passages of the demand for a sign should be regarded from an exodus typological persepective. They recall the *dor* of the Wilderness as a typos of 'this *genea*'. In the early Jewish pattern regarding evil, god-forsaking *dorot* in the history of the world and Israel, the aspect of judgement and the demand for repentance play a prominent roll. Ungodly *dorot* are struck by God's judgement. But - it is stressed time and time again - God gave a respite and delayed punishment so that man would have time to repent and thus avoid being scourged - see e.g. *Mek. Ex.* 15:6[92]. This is in fact the same pattern that we find regarding Jonah and the Ninevites, although the outcome differs from that in the ancient Jewish *dor* conceptions.

True, the term *dor/genea* is not used in that case. Instead there is mention of ἄνδρες Νινευῖται 'Ninevite men' (Mt 12:41 / Lk 11:32). But אנשי 'men' (const.) with the accompanying attribute is the expression used at the time when it, as here, refers to the inhabitants of a city.[93] A frequent example in the rabbis is אנשי סדום 'the men of Sodom'. They are mentioned frequently in parity with 'the *dor* of the Flood', 'the *dor* of the Wilderness' and other similar collectives.[94] In the *dor* conception in question the following pattern emerges: the wickedness of man - God's judgement - delay (ארכה) of the punishment that people might repent - their neglect of the opportunity to repent - the divine punishment. We find the same pattern regarding Jonah and the Ninevites, but the content is different on one decisive point: the wickedness of man - God's judgement, passed by Jonah - respite with the destruction of Nineveh (forty days, Jon 3:4) - the *repentance* of the Ninevites - God's *removal of the impending judgement* on the city. In contrast to other *dorot/geneai* and collectives the people of the heathen

---

[91] D. Daube, "'For they know not what they do': Luke 23,34", *Studia patristica* IV, 1961, 67 f.

[92] See further below p. 110 f.

[93] It can even be used in other circumstances; see below p. 39 f.

[94] See above p.11 n.18. The phrase אנשי נינוה 'the men of Nineveh' is not unusual in ancient Jewish literature (e.g. *m. Ta'an* 2:1; *Gen. Rab.* 44:12 [90b]; *Ex. Rab.* 45:1 [74a]), and it is undoubtedly here we have to look for the background to the gospel phrase. Cf. belove p. 39 f. regarding the expression 'the men of this *genea*' (Lk 7:31).

Nineveh listened to God's messenger and acted according to the message. They accepted Jonah's preaching - τὸ κήρυγμα 'Ιωνᾶ, Mt 12:41 par. Lk 11:32 - and were saved.

With his reference to Jonah and the Ninevites Jesus teaches his listeners what their attitude towards him ought to be: they were to accept his message, convert and be saved. But that is not what happened. And when he then contrasts the men of Nineveh to 'this *genea*' and says that they will 'condemn' it at the judgement, this corresponds to a well-documented model of thought in ancient Judaism. 'This *genea*' has not opened themselves to his preaching as the Ninevites did to Jonah's - in spite of the fact expressed in the statement πλεῖον 'Ιωνᾶ ὧδε (Mt 12:41 / Lk 11:32). Like the *dor* of the Wilderness at the first exodus they have instead cut themselves off and distanced themselves from the Saviour sent to them by God at the time of fulfilment (Mt 12:41a / Lk 11:32a).

In the double saying in Mt 12:41 f. par. Lk 11:31 f. it is not now only the men of Nineveh but also the Queen of the South[95] who is contrasted to 'this *genea*'. Why is she and her visit to Solomon mentioned here (cf.1 Kings 10:1-13 / 2 Chron 9:1-12)? Is the sole reason that she, in spite of her heathen origins, wished to hear words of wisdom from Solomon, which had, of course, come from God (cf. 1 Kings 5:9 / 4:29/)? Or can there be further reasons?

It is said that the Queen came from the ends of the earth to hear τὴν σοφίαν Σολομῶνος 'the wisdom of Solomon' (Mt 12:42 / Lk 11:31). In accordance with 1 Kings 5:9-14 (4:29-34) Solomon was seen in early Israel as the wise man *par excellence*. According to ancient Jewish belief he had even been given the knowledge how to drive out and subdue demons.[96] Our main witness from the first century AD is Josephus. He describes in *Ant* VIII, 2:5 § 42-49 Solomon's extensive wisdom - even greater than that of the Egyptians - and continues: "And God granted him knowledge of the art used against demons for the benefit and healing of men. He also composed incantations by which illnesses are relieved, and left behind forms of exorcisms with which those possessed by demons drive them out, never to return. And this kind of cure is of very great power among us to this day"...

This testimony to Solomon and his wisdom, used 'to this day', brings into focus the context in Mt 12 / Lk 11.[97] In both passages the matter

---

[95] The Queen of Sheba is here called βασίλισσα νότου 'the Queen of the South'. Cf. *Test. Sol.* 19:3 and 21:1, where she is called ἡ Σάβα βασίλισσα νότου and Σάβα ἡ βασίλισσα νότου respectively. Here Sheba has thus become a proper name.

[96] See D.C. Duling, *Testament of Solomon* in *OTP* I, 1983, 945–951.

of the sign can be found together with the Beelzebul controversy (Mt 12:22 ff. / Lk 11:14 ff.). In Lk the connection between them is quite clearly marked. The Beelzebul attack and the demand for a sign are to be found side by side in the beginning of the section (vs.15 f.). In Mt there is also an indication that they are connected, when it is said that Jesus' opponents 'answered' (ἀπεκρίθησαν) Jesus' preaching (starting in the Beelzebul conflict) with a wish to see a sign from him (v. 38).[98] They also belong together in a factual sense. The Beelzebul passage gives a concrete demonstration of the unbelieving attitude to Jesus' deeds that is expressed in the demand in question. In the tradition represented by Mt and Lk the two thus belong together.

In the Beelzebul pericope Jesus is accused by his antagonists of having cast out demons by Beelzebul. To this he answers: "If I cast out demons by Beelzebul, by whom do your sons cast them out? Therefore they shall be your judges" (Mt 12:27 / Lk 11:19). What can be meant by this? The information we have definitely leads to the conclusion that the Jewish exorcists indicated in this saying mainly used 'the art used against demons' which was assumed to come from Solomon. It was 'the wisdom of Solomon' they made use of.

Is it against this background that the saying about the Queen of the South in Mt 12:42 / Lk 11:31 is to be seen and understood? As regards this question we should pay attention to two further circumstances. 1) Even if Solomon received his wisdom from God, one must keep separate 'God's wisdom' and 'Solomon's wisdom'. While in several New Testament texts reference is made to God's wisdom, *Mt 12:42 and Lk 11:31 are the only passages where Solomon's wisdom is mentioned.* 2) When Josephus gives a historical picture of Solomon, he refers to his extraordinary wisdom. Thereby he stresses that God even taught him the art of gaining power over the demons. That was thus a central characteristic in the description of the king. In the continuation Josephus even describes the driving out of a devil, mentioning the name of Solomon and the use of his incantations, and concludes: through this "the understanding and wisdom of Solomon were clearly revealed, on account of which we have been induced to speak of these things, in

---

[97] Cf. E. Lövestam, "Jésus Fils de David chez les Synoptiques", *ST* 28, 1974, 97–109.

[98] As E. Schweizer puts it: "Die Zeichenfrage ist ... Lk. 11,16.29–32 eng mit der Beelzebulrede verwoben. Matthäus folgt also Q, wenn er sie hier einfügt" (*Das Evangelium nach Matthäus*, 1973, 188). The verb ἀπεκρίθησαν here apparently means 'answered' (and not just 'said'); cf. Th. Zahn, *Das Evangelium des Matthäus*, 1922, 467; W. Grundmann, *Das Evangelium des Matthäus*, 1968, 333; K. Stendahl, *Matthew* in *PCB*, 1962, 785; J. Gnilka, *Das Matthäusevangelium* I, 1986, 464; U. Luz, *Das Evangelium nach Matthäus* II, 1990, 275.

order that all men may know the greatness of his nature and how God favoured him" ... (*Ant* VIII, 2:5 § 49). *The highest expression of Solomon's wisdom was his ability to have power over the evil spirits.* Josephus clearly documents this as being the Jewish opinion of that time.

Jesus' reference to the Queen of Sheba and her interest in 'the wisdom of Solomon' ends with the proclamation: "Something greater than Solomon is here" (Mt 12:42 / Lk 11:31). It is not reasonable to suppose that in such a context there would be a reference to ἡ σοφία Σολομῶνος without thinking about that which in Jewish circles was considered the *highest* manifestation of this wisdom. This applies especially in this particular case if one takes into consideration 1) that the question of a sign both in Mt and Lk is, as stated above, connected with the Beelzebul controversy, which has Jesus' driving out of a demon as its starting point, 2) that Mk does not include the passage on the Jewish exorcists in the Beelzebul section (Mk 3:22 ff.) nor does he refer to the sign dialogue with Jesus' words about 'the wisdom of Solomon' in this context [99], and 3) that the pericope on the return of the unclean spirit in Mt (12:43-45) - ending with the statement, "So shall it be also with this evil *genea*" - follows immediately on the passage about Solomon, a fact which could support an orientation in the direction mentioned here.[100]

It thus turns out to be, in all probability, the central theme in the preceding Beelzebub controversy which is referred to in Jesus' saying about the visit of the Queen to hear 'the wisdom of Solomon' with its

---

[99] There is also a link between the two passages which is at least worth mentioning. When it is said of the Queen of the South that she will 'condemn' (κατακρινεῖ) 'this *genea*' this is admittedly a parallel to what is said in the double-word about the Ninevites. But it has also a certain affinity with what is said about the Jewish exorcists in the Beelzebul controversy:..."they shall be your judges (κριταί)" (Mt 12:27 / Lk 11:19).

It should also be noted that in *Test. Sol.* - where the Queen of Sheba is called βασίλισσα νότου (see above) just as she is in the Gospels - she is said to be a γόης, 'a witch' (19:3). This is also the case in later legends; cf. L. Ginzberg, *The Legends of the Jews* VI, 1928, 292 n. 55; M. Reiser, *Die Gerichtspredigt Jesu*, 1990, 198. This is something which could point in the same direction as that which has been mentioned above.

[100] In Lk the pericope in question comes before Jesus' answer to the demand for a sign (11:24-26). – Regarding the significance of the pericope cf. W.D. Davies - D.C. Allison, *op. cit.* II, 359 f., where different suggestions as to interpretation are also given. Its function in Mt is obviously to focus the seriousness and responsibility of the *genea* who have seen and heard the second Redeemer, greater than Jonah and greater than Solomon, but who have not opened themselves and received the gift of liberation. On 'this wicked *genea*' waits the worst of fates - according to Mt 12:41 f. Matthew has the last judgement in mind. Compare below with Mt 23:29-36 and par.

continuation, "Here is something greater than Solomon". In contrast to 'the art used against demons', which goes back to Solomon and is said to be the height of his wisdom, Jesus defeated the evil spirits by 'the Spirit of God'/'the finger of God' (Mt 12:28 / Lk 11:20) - note that the latter expression alludes to the exodus story (Ex 8:15 [8:19]). As the demons' activities are seen by the Synoptics to be expressed in illness, either mental or physical or both (cf. Mt 12:22 / Lk 11:14; Acts 10:38)[101], one can here compare with Jesus' answer to the disciples of John the Baptist (Mt 11:4 f. / Lk 7:21 f.).

With those implications of the references to Jonah/the Ninevites and Solomon/the Queen of the South respectively they represent the two main aspects of Jesus' activities: his preaching (NB Mk 1:14 f.) and his mighty works.

Both in relation to the prophet Jonah and to Solomon, Jesus emphasizes: ἰδοὺ πλεῖον Σολομῶνος ὧδε (Mt 12:41/Lk 11:31), ἰδοὺ πλεῖον Ἰωνᾶ ὧδε (Mt 12:41/Lk 11:32). The greatness of Jesus is expressed not in the masculine but in the neuter. We find here an indirect, 'open' christology which gives a strong impression of originality and authenticity.[102] In the meeting with Jesus people have been faced with something greater than Jonah and his κήρυγμα and demand for repentance, addressed to the men of Nineveh. And they have been faced with something greater than Solomon and his wisdom, even in its highest manifestation (see above), namely in Jesus' δυνάμεις. But the behaviour of people at the time of the first exodus has been repeated.

By using the two historical examples a perspective onwards is now opened. The emphasis on that which is 'greater' than Jonah and 'greater' than Solomon is part of an argumentation of *qal wa-chomer* type which applies to 'this *genea*'. The Ninevites repented on hearing Jonah preach, and the Queen of the South came to hear the wisdom of Solomon, how much more should not then ἡ γενεὰ αὕτη listen to Jesus and believe in him. But they did not, and therefore their judgement is waiting. We find in this saying the same pattern as when, in the above-mentioned Jewish motivation for the flight of Jonah, a fear is expressed that the repentant heathen Ninevites would be a condemnation on the unrepentant Israel: "At the judgement the men of Nineveh will stand up together with[103] this *genea* and 'condemn'[104] it"... And the same applies

---

[101] See E. Lövestam, *op. cit.*, 99 with ref.

[102] Cf. F. Mussner, "Wege zum Selbstbewusstsein Jesu", *BZ* NF 12, 1968, 170 f.; M. Reiser, *Die Gerichtspredigt Jesu*, 1990, 202 f., 205 f. (with argumentation and ref.). W.D. Davies – D.C. Allison ask: "... can we not understand πλεῖον to cover the 'Christ-event' in general? That is, can it not be equated with the coming of the kingdom and its herald, Jesus?" (*op. cit.*, 358).

to the Queen of the South.

As was stated above, the *dorot* in question and comparable collectives (e.g. 'the men of Sodom') are looked on and treated as units even in an eschatological sense.[105] This is also the case here. At the judgement 'this *genea*' will be condemned, as it has the character of a wicked *genea*. This is underlined by the accompanying adjective πονηρός 'evil' (Mt 12:39, 45; 16:4; Lk 11:29) and μοιχαλίς 'adulterous' (Mt 12:39; 16:4) - the last-mentioned term has, of course, its background in the prophetic aspect of the relationship between God and the people as an engagement or a marriage (e.g. Hos 2:2 ff.; Ezek 16:1 ff.; Is 1:21; Jer 3:3) and is thus an expression of qualified faithlessness to the God of the covenant. But it is not the people of Israel as such that are referred to, in contrast to the heathens.[106] A limitation to a particular epoch is clearly seen in the texts. Based on what has come forth earlier, however, what is intended is not days and years, not a 'quantitative' limitation in that sense. The perspective is salvation-historical. The limitation is linked to the appearance and preaching and deeds of Jesus. The term applies to those who, through Jesus, have experienced God's work among his people to a greater extent than earlier (πλεῖον...ὧδε), from the aspect of fulfilment, but closed themselves

---

[103] The Greek expression (ἀνίστασθαι μετά and ἐγείρεσθαι μετά respectively) "may simply mean 'will rise from the dead' along with; but it may also reflect the Hebrew/Aramaic legal expression *qwm 'm*, 'stand up with,' i.e. to take the position of an accuser, if the expression attested in rabbinic writings be also contemporary" (J. Fitzmyer, *The Gospel According to Luke* II, 1985, 936). Under all circumstances it must be the last judgement which is meant; NB the definite article (ἐν τῇ κρίσει), which shows that it is referring to a particular reality, well-known to the listener/reader (M. Reiser, *Die Gerichtspredigt Jesu*, 1990, 196–198), and the use of ἐγείρεσθαι as a variation of ἀνίστασθαι (e.g. J. Gnilka, *Das Matthäusevangelium* I, 1986, 467; U. Luz, *Das Evangelium nach Matthäus* II, 1990, 280). Cf. the expression עוֹמְדִין בְּדִין about the *dor* of the Flood, the *dor* of the Wilderness et al. in *m. Sanh.* 10:3.

[104] Κατακρίνειν = חִיֵּב, 'to prove to be in the wrong', 'to bring down condemnation'; see above p. 30. Cf. Heb 11:7: "By faith Noah, being warned by God concerning events as yet unseen, took heed and constructed an ark for the saving of his household; by this he condemned (κατέκρινεν) the world". As M. Reiser states (*op. cit.*, 204), the phrase κατακρίνειν ἐν τῇ κρίσει has a direct Semitic counterpart in the combination of בדין and חיב in *'Abot R. Nat.* 6 (20b): "In the future, at Judgement (בדין), R. Akiba will put all the poor in a guilty light (חייב). For if they are asked, 'Why did you not study Torah?' and they say, 'Because we were poor,' they shall be told: 'Indeed, was not Rabbi Akiba even poorer and in more wretched circumstances!' And if they say, 'Because of our children,' they shall be asked, 'And did not Rabbi Akiba have sons and daughters?'"

[105] Above p. 16.

[106] For this interpretation see e.g. D. Lührmann, *Die Redaktion der Logienquelle*, 1969, 30 f., 32–43.

to the revelation and reacted with doubt and unfaithfulness.

In Mt 12:41 f. / Lk 11:31 f. the eschatological judgement of ἡ γενεὰ αὕτη is clearly emphasized. With reference to the roles of the Ninevites and the Queen of the South it is stated that 'this *genea*' will be 'condemned'. How then should this saying be understood? In the light of the *dor* terminology in early Jewish writings there are two important aspects here. Firstly as noted above it is characteristic of the concept in question that God gives a respite (ארכה) before he lets judgement fall, so that people will be able to repent. This also happens to the Ninevites according to the book of Jonah, and when they repent God stops the punishment - even though it is not implied that he would do so when the judgement is passed (Jon 3:5-10).[107] Secondly a wicked *dor/genea* is a qualitatively homogeneous unit, which people can separate themselves from, thus avoiding being struck by the impending punishment.[108] This must also apply in this case. Jesus' words are then a serious warning both to 'this *genea*' as a whole and to each individual with the meaning: repent!

---

[107] See above p. 29–32. and cf. p. 28 n. 81.
[108] See above p. 13–17.

4. A Parable about ἡ γενεά αὕτη

Jesus' parable of the playing children (Mt 11:16–19 par. Lk 7:31–35) can be found in the same context in both Mt and Lk. It is part of the larger section about Jesus and John the Baptist in Mt 11:2–19 par. Lk 7:18–35. In both Gospels this passage begins with the question John sends from his prison to Jesus regarding his mission, and Jesus' answer. After that follows his testimony to the Baptist, and finally there is the parable of 'this *genea*' and its application.[109] It thus concerns a section where the idea of the fulfilment of the Scriptures is strongly marked, emphasized as it is in the question posed by John's disciples and in Jesus' answer, as well as in his witness about John's role and identity.

Regarding the mission and identity of Jesus, his *dynameis* play a major role in both the Synoptics. In Mt 11 the section is introduced in v. 2 with a reference to them. When John heard in prison about 'the deeds of the Christ', he sent his disciples to him with the question, if Jesus was 'the coming One' (ὁ ἐρχόμενος). And when it is said in v. 19 that wisdom is justified ἀπὸ τῶν ἔργων αὐτῆς (Lk: ἀπὸ πάντων τῶν τέκνων αὐτῆς), Matthew apparently associates to τὰ ἔργα τοῦ Χριστοῦ in the beginning of the paragraph and thus achieves an inclusio. The emphasis on the deeds is further underlined by the fact that our section is immediately followed by Jesus' woes on the impenitent Galilean cities.[110] There Jesus refers to the mighty works (δυνάμεις) which he had carried out in Chorazin, Bethsaida and Capernaum – however, these towns did not repent (vs. 20–24).

As in Mt the section in Lk is also introduced with a reference to Jesus' deeds. In chap. 7:1 ff. it tells how he cured the centurion's servant and raised the widow's son in Nain and after that follows the presentation in question: the disciples of the Baptist told him 'of all these things' (περὶ πάντων τούτων), and then John called to him two of them and sent them to Jesus with the question about his mission. It is also emphasized that at that very time Jesus cured many who had diseases, plagues and evil spirits, and gave sight to many who were blind (vs. 18 ff.).

---

[109] There is thus a far-reaching agreement between Matthew's version and that of Luke, apart from Mt 11:12–15 (cf. Lk 16:16) and Lk 7:29 f. (cf. Mt 21:31 f.). – As for the differences in wording between Mt and Lk regarding the parable and its application, see e.g. O. Linton, "The Parable of the Children's Game", *NTS* 22, 1976, 160–171.

[110] In Lk these woes are in another context (10:13–15).

The reason why the Baptist sent messengers to Jesus was thus, according to both Gospels, the mighty deeds he hade carried out. Jesus' answer is that they should go and tell John only what they hear and see. His way of expressing this is replicated in an almost identical manner in Mt and Lk: "the blind receive their sight and the lame walk, lepers are cleansed and the deaf hear, and the dead are raised up, and the poor have good news preached to them" (Mt 11:5 par. Lk 7:22). It is fundamental, of course, that this summary of what John's disciples hear and see happen through Jesus is a free rendering of Old Testament sayings about God's future acts of salvation (Is 35:5 f.; 29:18 f.; 61:1).[111] This implies that the prophetic promises – regarded as referring to eschatological blessings – are seen to be fulfilled in Jesus' actions. His *dynameis* are signs in that context, i.e. for those who can see the signs.

After giving his answer to John's messengers, Jesus turns to the crowds and speaks to them about John and gives his testimony to him. He witnesses that the Baptist is "more than a prophet" and that "there is not a mother's son greater than John" (Lk 7:26,28 par. Mt 11:9,11). He is the forerunner, who has come to fulfil the prophecy in Mal 3:1 (cf. Ex 23:20; Mk 1:2; Mt 11:10 par. Lk 7:27).[112]

In John the Baptist and Jesus the instruments of fulfilment are thus present and active among the people. What about the reactions to their appearance and activity? That is what Jesus describes in the following, and here comes the parable where 'this *genea*' is focused: "To what shall I compare τὴν γενεὰν ταύτην?" (Mt 11:16). Instead of the simple *genea*-formula Lk has τοὺς ἀνθρώπους τῆς γενεᾶς ταύτης, 'the men of this *genea*' (Lk 7:31). This has given rise to different interpretations.[113] Luke's mode of expression has, however, its coun-

---

[111] Cf. J. Jeremias, *Jesus' Promise to the Nations*, 1967, 45 f.; P. Hoffmann, *Studien zur Theologie der Logienquelle* , 1972, 204 f. As J. Fitzmyer puts it: "Rather than understanding his mission as that of a fiery reformer of the eschaton, Jesus sees his role as the embodiment of the divine blessings promised to be shed on the unfortunate of human society by Isaiah" (*The Gospel according to Luke* I, 1982, 664).

[112] Cf. E. Käsemann, *Essays on New Testament Themes*, 1964, 42 f.: ..."the Old Testament epoch of salvation history concludes with the Baptist, who himself already belongs to the new epoch".

[113] Luke has been found to write "individualisierend" (H. Schürmann, *Das Lukas-evangelium* I, 1969, 423) or as "a reaction against a too collective conception of responsibility" (O. Linton, "The Parable of the Children's game", *NTS* 22, 1976, 160 f.) or "stressing the serious situation of *men* who behave no better than *children*" (I.H. Marshall, *The Gospel of Luke*, 1978, 300) or underlining the sense of 'this *genea*' as "the sum total of those born at the same time, comtemporaries" (C.F. Evans, *Saint Luke*, 1990, 357), etc. O. Linton says that τοὺς ἀνθρώπους in Lk 7:31

terpart in many places in post-biblical Jewish literature when the text deals with different *dorot* (*geneai*): *m. B. Mes.* 4:2 (אנשי דור המבול) side by side with the simple (דור הפלגה), *b. Sanh.* 38b (אנשי דור המבול ואנשי דור) (הפלגה), *3 Enoch* 7 (בני דור המבול), etc. There is scarcely any substantial difference between Mt and Lk on this point.[114]

When in the section at hand Jesus' *dynameis* play a central role in this way we find ourselves within a problem area that has affinity with the questions in the texts of the demand for a sign.[115] There can hardly be any doubt that the γενεά concept has the same meaning here as in that case. For the Old Testament background, reference has at times been made to Ps 95:10[116] – note the role this passage with its context plays in Heb 3:7–4:11. Admittedly in the Psalm text the pronoun in the *dor* formula is missing in MT, but LXX, Hier., Syr. read בַּדּוֹר הַהוּא, and when the passage is quoted in Heb 3:10 the expression is rendered in the incomparably best text tradition by ἡ γενεὰ αὕτη.[117] The uncertainty regarding the formulation should not therefore be regarded as an obstacle to a connection with this Psalm passage in the parable. There are, however, also other OT texts that can be referred to, e.g. Deut 32:5; Ps 78:8.[118]

The question is whether there is anything in the conception of godless *dorot/geneai* in ancient Israel and particularly in that of the *dor* of the Wilderness that can have special relevance for the parable of the Children's Game.

The meaning of this parable has been much discussed.[119] It has

"in any case is secondary" (*op. cit.*, 163), but that cannot be taken for granted in the light of the early Jewish terminology.

[114] NB how both the expressions οἱ ἄνδρες τῆς γενεᾶς ταύτης and ἡ γενεὰ αὕτη are paralled in Lk 11:31,32. Cf above p. 31 about 'the men of Nineveh'. – As for Jesus' question what 'this *genea*' may be *compared* to, cf. the rabbinic explanation that just before the advent of the Messiah the face of the *dor* will *be like* the face of a dog (כִּפְנֵי הַכֶּלֶב), i.e. impervious to shame; *m. Sota* 9:15.

[115] Cf. above p. 24 f.

[116] So e.g.. A. Polag, *Die Christologie der Logienquelle,* 1977, 89; 138; S. Légasse, "L'oracle contra 'cette génération'", *Logia*, ed. J. Delobel (BETL 59), 1982, 246 f.

[117] LXX has ἡ γενεὰ ἐκείνη. Cf. below p. 99.

[118] Cf. above p. 22 n. 60 and V.Hasler sub γενεά in *EWNT*.

[119] See e.g. C.H. Dodd, *The Parables of the Kingdom,* rev. ed. 1961, 15 f.; J. Jeremias, *Die Gleichnisse Jesu,* 4. Aufl. 1956, 139-141; M. Hermaniuk, *La Parabole Evangélique,* 1947, 200-203; F. Mussner, "Der nicht erkannte Kairos (Mt 11,16-19 = Lk 7,31-35)", *Bib* 40, 1959, 599-612; H. Schürmann, *Das Lukasevangelium* I, 1969, 421–429; O. Linton, "The Parable of the Children's Game", *NTS* 22, 1976, 159-179; P. Hoffmann, *Studien zur Theologie der Logienquelle,* 1972, 224-231; D. Zeller, "Die Bildlogik des Gleichnisses Mt 11,16f. / Lk 7,31f.", *ZNW* 68, 1977,

rightly been looked on as a *crux interpretum*. The simile is about children sitting in a market-place (Lk; Mt: in the market-places) who want to play at weddings and at funerals respectively but in neither case do their comrades want to join in. Therefore they reproach them (Mt 11:16 f. par. Lk 7:31 f.). How is this related to 'this *genea*' and how is it to be understood from this perspective?

The most common view is that 'this *genea*' is compared with the children who are addressed in the parable.[120] Those who have invited them to play (at weddings and funerals respectively) are then identified with John the Baptist and Jesus. John, the ascetic, talked about judgment and called for mourning and repentance, while Jesus ate and drank with the tax-collectors and sinners and offered people a share in the joy of the kingdom of heaven. But both were denied by '(the men of) this *genea*'. As has been pointed out by several scholars this interpretation is, however, associated with some serious problems.[121] It is not compatible with the introduction to the parable where 'this *genea*' is likened to the addressing children.[122] And the order between the two invitations to play (first to dance and then to mourn) does not correspond to the actual chronology: first John and then Jesus. Furthermore the children of the parable who speak (λέγουσιν) their complaint in Mt 11:17 (with par.) are like those who speak (λέγουσιν[123]) their reproach in vs. 18 and 19 ('He has a demon', 'Behold a glutton'...), i.e. the people of 'this *genea*'. There is thus good reason to question this explanation.

Another interpretation sees 'this *genea*' as likened not to the children spoken to but to those who propose the games.[124] It connects to the

252-257; W. Cotter, "The Parable of the Children in the Market-place, Q (Lk) 7:31-35: An Examination of the Parable's Image and Significance", *NovT* 29, 1987, 289-304; U. Luz, *Das Evangelium nach Matthäus* II, 1990, 184–188; W.D. Davies - D.C. Allison, *A Critical and Exegetical Commentary on the Gospel according to Saint Matthew* II, 1991, 259-265.

[120] Mt's ἑτέροις is usually given preference to Lk's ἀλλήλοις (Mt 11:16 / Lk 7:32). It is difficult to determine what is really meant by the Lukan expression here. What is focused is anyhow the address (προσφωνεῖν) with the complaint that the presumtive playmates have not followed the signals but refused to conform to the given proposals. Cf. M.-J. Lagrange, *Evangile selon Saint Luc*, 1948, 223; H. Schürmann, *op. cit.*, 423–425.

[121] Cf. U. Luz, *op. cit.*, 184 f.; W.D. Davies-D.C. Allison, *op. cit.*, 261 f.

[122] Cf. U. Luz, who points out that in this interpretation the introduction is not only, as often was the case in Jewish parables, "ungenau, sondern gerade verkehrt, denn sie vergleicht ausdrücklich diese Generation mit den ansperchenden Kindern" (*op. cit.*, 185).

[123] Lk has λέγετε here (7:33 f.).

[124] E.g. Th. Zahn, *Das Evangelium des Matthäus*, 1922, 432; E. Percy, *Die Bot-*

introduction to the parable and has to that extent a significant basis. The order in the parable with the children first being called upon to dance and then to mourn is also in accordance chronologically with the application which first mentions John, the ascete, and thereafter the joyful Jesus. The most common objection to this view is that John and Jesus must correspond to the *active* children, 'this *genea*' to the *passive* and unwilling children. O. Linton notes that and continues, "This idea seemed so self-evident that most scholars felt themselves obliged to dismiss the introduction as a bad or even misleading arrangement".[125]

The question arises how this interpretation is to be looked on in the light of the ἡ γενεὰ αὕτη conception as it has emerged here. Then two factors become interesting.

It is first a recurring characteristic in the picture of an evil *dor/genea* that it does not merely passively disregard those who are sent by God to their help and salvation. It is *active* against them. That is patently the case regarding the most relevant conception here, the *dor* of the Wilderness. As has been seen above, the Israel of the exodus did not comply with the terms of the liberation, as they were expressed under the leadership of Moses. And they made their views clear. They reacted against Moses (and Aaron) and thus against God. In spite of all the *dynameis* God had let take place through his instruments at the deliverance, they did not believe but complained and reproached, finally with tragic results. Even in Ps 95:8–10 this is emphasized (cf. above).

In consideration of the wording of the parable it should further be pointed out that it is frequently said in the exodus texts that the people *spoke against* Moses (and Aaron) and the Lord. In descriptions of the challenging opposition of the wanderers in the desert this is emphasized time and time again. As in Num 21 about the opposition of the *dor* of the Wilderness described there, which led to the punishment with the snakes: the people "spoke against God and against Moses, 'why have you brought us up out of Egypt to die in the wilderness?...' ", and after the Lord's punishment they confessed to Moses: "We have sinned, for we have spoken against the Lord and against you..." (vs. 5, 7). The same is true of several other passages, e.g. in Num 20:3: "The people con-

schaft Jesu, 1953, 251–253; J. Jeremias, *Die Gleichnisse Jesu*, 1956, 139 f.; I.H. Marshall, *The Gospel of Luke*, 1978, 300 f.; O. Linton, *op. cit.*, 159–179; W.D. Davies-D.C. Allison, *op. cit.*, 261 f.

[125] See *op. cit.*, 176 f. and Linton's comments there. – According to a third type of interpretation 'this *genea*' is not represented by one or other of the two categories of children but by all, the entire group, which together exhibit their character and attitude. The *tertium comparationis* can then be understood in different ways. Cf. P. Hoffmann, *op. cit.*, 224–227; U. Luz, *op. cit.*, 186.

tended with Moses and said"... It is interesting to note that the central place-name in that context, *Meribah* (from Hebr. ריב, 'contend'; see Ex 17:1–7) in the Septuagint is usually given as (/τὸ/ ὕδωρ) ἀντιλογίας, '(the water of) contradiction' (Num 20:13; 27:14; Deut 32:51; 33:8; Ps 80:8 /81:8/; 105:32 /106:32/).

In Ex 17:7 and Num 20:24, however, *Meribah* and '*the waters of Meribah*' are rendered in the LXX by Λοιδόρησις and τὸ ὕδωρ τῆς λοιδορίας respectively. That corresponds to the fact that Hebr. ריב ('contend') – which in the Greek Bible otherwise is rendered with a variety of verbs (μάχεσθαι, κρίνειν etc.) – with reference to the people's opposition in the wilderness is consistently given with the otherwise unusual equivalent λοιδορεῖν, 'revile, abuse' (Ex 17:2; Num 20:3,13 etc.). The root λοιδορ- thus marks an emphasis on the element of revilement in the oppositional behaviour of the *dor* of the desert.

Other terms that may be mentioned are e.g. Hebr. נאץ, 'despise, flout' (LXX: παροξύνειν) – "how long will this people despise me?" the Lord asks in Num 14:11, and the same verb recurs in v. 23 –, נאץ (*Hif.*), 'anger' (LXX: παροργίζειν), as in Ps 106:32 /105:32/: "They angered him at the waters of Meribah".

Against this background the 'this *genea*' concept fits well into the introduction of the parable according to which ἡ γενεὰ αὕτη is likened to the addressing children. In the context in Mt 11/Lk 7 it is, as has been seen above, strongly marked that it deals with the time of fulfilment. With John the Baptist as the forerunner, Jesus was the fulfiller of God's promises in the Scriptures for the time to come. But the two did not work in a vacuum. Like 'the first deliverer' at the first exodus they were active among living people, who had their expectations and put their terms. Pharisees and others who decisively influenced the opinions of 'this *genea*' certainly had their ideas and hopes as to what the deliverance of the OT promises was about and how it would take place.[126] They also had their ideas about the instruments of

---

[126] Cf. those involved in the texts of the demand for a sign: the scribes and Pharisees (Mt 12:38), the Pharisees and Sadducees (Mt 16:1), the Pharisees (Mk 8:11). There were of course also those who listened to John and Jesus. In Lk 7:29 f. it is even said that all (πᾶς) the people, including the toll-collectors, had listened to John and accepted his baptism in contrast to the Pharisees and the lawyers (cf. Mt 21:32) – cf. Luke's generalising mode of expression e.g. in Acts 10:38 (Jesus went about "healing all /πάντας/ that were opressed by the devil") and Acts 19:10 (Paul was active in Ephesus for two years, "so that all /πάντας/ the residents of Asia heard the words of the Lord, both Jews and Greeks"). With that generalisation in Lk 7:29 the Pharisees and lawyers are presented in a correspondingly much more negative fashion. In connection with the saying about them in v. 30 is the parable presented in vs. 31–35.

God who were to carry out the task. But John and Jesus did not meet these expectations. They did not follow the given signals but broke with the current pattern. Therefore they were both opposed and reproached by 'this *genea*', an opposition which is expressed in the parable in the category of 'speaking against'... (Mt 11:18 f. par. Lk 7:33 f.).

In the application the accusations are made concrete. The attacks on Jesus for being 'a glutton and a drunkard, a friend of tax collectors and sinners' (Mt 11:19/Lk 7:34) recall the Pharisees' imputation against him for sharing a table with tax gatherers and sinners in Mt 9:10–13/Lk 5:29–32/Mk 2:15–17 (cf. Lk 15:2; 19:7), an imputation that he counters by referring to the very purpose of his task: "I have not come to call the righteous, but sinners" (Mt 9:14–17/Lk 5:33–39/Mk 2:18–22).[127] As to the Baptist we have no clear evidence in this respect, but see the note about his clothing and food in Mt 3:4 (Mk 1:6; cf. Lk 1:15).

This then means that the central element of the parable is *the reproach*. That is also, in fact, apparent in the text. One can speculate as to the specific relationship between the two groups of children. Are they boys in the one case and girls in the other, etc.? But it is the children's remarks that are in focus. And that means not just a description of what has happened. It has the function of a complaint, a reproach. That is what is emphasized. The application to the behaviour of the people towards John and Jesus is also in complete agreement with this.

Concerning the allusions to Israel in the wilderness a further comment may be made. In a concluding sentence in connection with the application of the parable, Jesus says: καὶ ἐδικαιώθη ἡ σοφία ἀπὸ τῶν ἔργων (Lk: πάντων τῶν τέκνων) αὐτῆς (Mt 11:19 par. Lk 7:35). Without dealing with this much discussed passage more closely we can note that wisdom is here referred to in contrast to the attitude of 'this *genea*'. Even in this case the Old Testament orientation is of interest. There are OT texts where the character and attitude that are typical for the *dor* of the Wilderness are depicted as being the opposite of wisdom. It is thus said in the Song of Moses in Deut 32 about Israel in the desert that it is 'a perverse and crooked *dor*' and in this connection it is asked: "Is this how you repay the Lord, you foolish and unwise people?" – 'unwise', חָכָם לֹא, LXX: οὐχὶ σοφός (Deut 32:5 f.; cf. v. 28 f.). In Ps 95:10[128] this characteristic is also emphasized. After the passage about the *dor* with which the Lord was indignant for forty years he says:

As for the rejection of John the Baptist by the people's spiritual leaders, see also Mt 21:32.

[127] U. Luz rightly points out: "Der Vorwurf, Jesus sei ein Fresser und Weinsäufer und Freund der Zöllner und Sünder, trifft ins Zentrum der Sendung Jesu" (*op. cit.*, 188).

[128] See above p. 40.

"They are a people who err in heart, and they will not discern my ways". Thus the above mentioned contrast does not either lack connections with the Old Testament picture of דור המדבר.

It should be noted that in Mt 11:16–19 par. John the Baptist and Jesus are placed side by side in relation to 'this *genea*'. It is said of both that he 'came' (ἦλθεν, Mt 11:18 f.) and 'has come' (ἐλήλυθεν, Lk 7:33 f.) respectively.[129] They belong together as the precursor and the fulfiller of the OT promises. When 'this *genea*' in the text is given its content and qualities in relation to both of them in that way, the salvation-historical character of this concept is clearly indicated.

In its exodus-typological perspective the phrase ἡ γενεὰ αὕτη certainly has a negative, portenteous tone, implying a warning of coming destruction and demands for repentance. In the Matthean context this is further underlined when the section in question is immediately followed by Jesus' woes on the Galilean cities in which so many of his δυνάμεις had been performed but which did not repent and were therefore on their way towards eschatological judgment (Mt 11:20–24).

---

[129] As for the different grammatical forms see O. Linton, *op. cit.*, 162 f.

5. The Pericope of the epileptic Boy

In all the Synoptics it is said that Jesus, on his descent from the mount of Transfiguration, is met by the scene with the epileptic boy whom the disciples could not heal but whom Jesus liberated from an evil spirit (Mk 9:14-29 par. Mt 17:14-20, Lk 9:37-43a). The description of this event has a similar structure in the three Gospels, but there are several differences otherwise, above all in Mk and Mt/Lk. Among other things, in the latter the notice about Jesus and the three disciples meeting the crowd and lawyers in discussion is missing (Mk 9:14b-16), as is the second description of the boy's condition, the dialogue between the father and Jesus about the power of faith and the mention of the boy's reactions on being cured in Mk 9:21-27.[130] Common to all the Synoptics is, however, that Jesus, on meeting the crowd with the father and the sick child and the helpless disciples, exclaims, with small differences in the formulation: "O unbelieving (Mt/Lk: and perverse) *genea*, how long shall I be with you[131]? How long[132] must I endure you?" (Mk 9:19 par. Mt 17:17; Lk 9:41).

The adjective ἄπιστος ('unbelieving') is added to γενεά in the texts

---

[130] At times it has been assumed that the version in Mk is the result of a combination of two stories (cf. P.J. Achtemeier, "Miracles and the Historical Jesus: A Study of Mark 9:14–29", *CBQ* 37, 1975, 471–491 with ref.). The structure of the pericope in Mk can, however, be explained satisfactorally without such an assumption (cf. G. Theissen, *Urchristliche Wundergeschichten*, 1974, 139 f.; R. Pesch, *Das Markusevangelium* II, 1977, 86, 95; U. Luz, *Das Evangelium nach Matthäus* II, 1990, 520). – Regarding matters of sources, tradition and redaction in this case see further e.g. K. Kertelge, *Die Wunder Jesu im Markusevangelium*, 1970, 174–179; W. Schenk, "Tradition und Redaktion in der Epileptiker-Perikope Mk 9,14–29", *ZNW* 63, 1972, 76–94; G. Petzke, "Die historische Frage nach den Wundertaten Jesu. Dargestellt am Beispiel des Exorzismus Mark. IX.14–29 Par", *NTS* 22, 1976, 180–204; H. Aichinger, "Zur Traditionsgeschichte der Epileptiker-Perikope Mk 9,14–29 par Mt 17,14–21 par Lk 9,37–43a" in A. Fuchs (ed.), *Studien zum NT und seiner Umwelt* Ser. A Bd 3, 1978, 114–143; U. Luz, *op. cit.*, 519–521; Christopher D. Marshall, *Faith as a Theme in Mark's Narrative*, 1989, 111-115; F. Bovon, *Das Evangelium nach Lukas*, 1989, 507 f.; W.D. Davies-D.C. Allison, *A Critical and Exegetical Commentary on the Gospel according to Saint Matthew* II, 1991, 719–721; G.E. Sterling, "Jesus as Exorcist: An Analysis of Matthew 17:14-20; Mark 9:14-29; Luke 9:37-43a", *CBQ* 55, 1993, 467-493 (where there is a detailed analysis of the pericope in the three Synoptics).

[131] Mk and Lk: πρὸς ὑμᾶς, Mt: μεθ' ὑμῶν.

[132] Lk has linked this clause with the previous one: "How long shall I be with you and endure you?" (9:41).

here, and in Mt/Lk διεστραμμένη ('perverse') as well.[133] The latter is to be found in the Song of Moses (Deut 32), where the faithless Israelites in the wilderness are called (LXX) γενεὰ σκολιὰ καὶ διεστραμμένη ('a crooked and perverse *dor/genea*', v. 5; cf. Phil 2:15). Σκολιός in this OT phrase is replaced in the gospel texts by ἄπιστος. That is the only passage in the New Testament where that adjective is used with γενεά. It indicates the importance of faith in that context.[134] However, this qualification can also be found in the same chapter in Deut, that is in v. 20, where the people are said to be 'a perverse (LXX: ἐξεστραμμένη) *dor/genea*, sons in whom there is no faithfulness (LXX: υἱοὶ οἷς οὐκ ἔστιν πίστις ἐν αὐτοῖς)' (Deut 32:20).[135] It is clear that the formulation in Mt/Lk refers to these passages about the people of the exodus.[136] Thus the expression used recalls the circumstances of the desert-wandering. And that takes place through the Poem of Moses in Deut 32, a fact which is worth noting and returning to.

It should also be noted that the pericope in question is combined in the Gospels with an account with marked exodus typological characteristics, namely the Transfiguration on the mountain.[137] That is the case in all three Synoptics. It is thus a stable synoptic tradition. As regards the combination between the two accounts it should be taken into consideration that the pericope about the epileptic boy presupposes an occasion when Jesus was absent.[138] Contextually our narrative is thus

---

[133] In a few mss (mainly P45vid) διεστραμμένη is also to be found in the Markan text.

[134] See e.g. Ch.D. Marshall's analysis of the Markan text; *op. cit.*, 110-123.

[135] Cf. F. Büchsel, γενεά κτλ., *TWNT* 1, 661. - As was noted above it refers to the *dor* of the Wilderness; cf. Freedman-Lundbom, דור *dôr* in *TWAT* I, 1974, 194: "Diese Generation war in der Geschichte Israels wohlbekannt; die Überlieferung ihrer Taten wurde zu einem festen Bestandteil der Lieder. Sie ist das Hauptthema in Deut 32 (vgl. v. 5. 20)..."

[136] Cf. D. Tabachovitz, *Die Septuaginta und das Neue Testament*, 1956, 114. H. Frankemölle states: "Da von den Auslegern in 17,17 par 9,41 die Wendung ὦ γενεὰ (ἄπιστος) καὶ διεστραμμένη übereinstimmend sprachlich auf das Moseslied am Ende des Dt (32,5.20) zurückgeführt wird, braucht dies hier lediglich bestätigt zu werden" (*Jahwebund und Kirche Christi*, 1974, 24).

[137] The Transfiguration pericope is certainly full of symbols. Its different motifs are to a certain extent multivalent and allow several possible associations. For a thorough treatment of the motifs of the account see H. Riesenfeld, *Jésus transfiguré*, 1947. It is clear that there is an important path of allusions to the Sinai theophany at the first exodus; cf. I.H. Marshall, *op. cit.*, 382 ff.; E.E. Ellis. *op. cit.*, 142; U. Luz, *op. cit.*, 507–509 ("Am wichtigsten sind ... die aus der Sinai-Theophanie übernommenen Züge ... und der Inthronisationsgedanke"; p. 509).

coupled to the Transfiguration story.

With that context, associations in an exodus perspective go primarily to the account in Ex 32: When Moses comes down from mount Sinai, where he met God in his glory and received the law tablets of the covenant, he finds the people in their lack of faith, dancing and singing before the bull-calf that had been moulded.

Here is then reason to return to the terminological connection to Deut 32:5,20 in Jesus' saying. The faithfulness of the Lord is contrasted, according to ancient Jewish interpretations, with the faithlessness of his people in turning to idolatry. Their corruption is referred to in v. 5 as 'their defect' (מוּמָם). In *Tg. Onq.* that is defined as idolatry: God is 'the faithful God', he is 'just and true'; "corruption is theirs, not His; children *who worship idols*, a דרא that changes its work, and has itself become changed". With the conception of idolatry during the wandering in the desert, its most tangible manifestation certainly comes to the fore, namely the moulding and worship of the golden calf.[139] In connection with vs. 20 f. the orientation in that direction in ancient Jewish literature is clearly expressed. After the statement that the people are 'a perverse *dor*' (γενεὰ ἐξεστραμμένη) it is, as is noted above, added appositionally in MT: 'sons in whom there is no faithfulness'. In the commentary on this passage in *Sipre Deut.* the incident of the golden calf is referred to primarily : "You are children in whom there is no constancy. You stood at mount Sinai and said, 'All that the Lord hath spoken will we do, and obey' (Ex 24:7). I responded, 'You are godlike beings' (Ps 82:6); but when you said about the golden calf, 'This is thy god, O Israel' (Ex 32:4), I said to you, 'Nevertheless, ye shall die like men' (Ps 82:7)" (*Sipre Deut.§* 320 [137a]).[140] There is thus an association to be

---

[138] Cf. J. Gnilka about the account of the healing: "Zu beachten ist die vorausgesetzte Abwesenheit Jesu, die ihre Einordnung an dieser Stelle im Evangelium möglich machte" (*Das Matthäusevangelium* II, 1988, 110; cf. P. Pesch, *Das Markusevangelium* II, 1977, 84).

[139] As I. Drazin puts it: *Tg. Onq.* "explains that in this verse Moses is reminding the people of the first of the Ten Commandments and is chastising them for their first sin, worshipping the golden calf" (*Targum Onkelos to Deuteronomy*, 1982, 271). Cf. B. Grossfeld, who refers to *Ex. Rab.* 42:1 (70a): "...When God saw this, He said to Moses: 'Go down, for your people ... have dealt corruptly (*schicheth*)'. The word *schicheth* signifies that they acted corruptly, as in the text ... (Deut 32:5). Not only /did/ they make an idol"... (*The Targum Onqelos to Deuteronomy*, 1988, 90).

[140] Cf. H.W. Basser, *Midraschic Interpretations of the Song of Moses*, 1984, 195. Basser remarks that the homily exists here in a similar way to the presentation of Justin Martyr (*Dialogue with Trypho*, chap. 132; 20–21;119) and assumes that the passage antedates the Christian polemic with this argumentation: "Would Jews use an anti-Jewish polemic unless this existed before Christians used it against Jews" (*op. cit.*,

48

found in ancient Jewish writings between the passages in the Song of Moses from which the phraseology in Mk 9:19 par. Mt 17:17; Lk 9:41 has been taken, and the narrative about the golden calf in Ex 32.

This sin of the people also played a prominent role in the complex of conceptions about the Israel of the first exodus. Among the rabbis it could quite simply be referred to as 'that deed'.[141] Cf. *Midr. Ps.* 1 § 14 (7a), where the words in Ps 1:1 about walking in the counsel of the wicked and standing in the way of sinners are applied to the *dor* of the Wilderness and their actions in connection with the golden calf:

> "'Blessed is the man who walks not in the counsel of the wicked'. This refers to the tribe of Levi who walked not in the counsel of the *dor* of the Wilderness, nor took part with them in the making of the golden calf; 'nor stands in the way of sinners', of whom it is said: 'Oh, this people have sinned a great sin, and have made for themselves gods of gold' (Ex 32:31). 'Nor sits in the seat of scoffers' (Ps 1:1), as it says: 'And the people (after making the golden calf) sat down to eat and drink, and rose up to play' (Ex 32:6)."[142]

In the New Testament too the manifest place of the worship of the calf in reference to the *dor* of the Wilderness is reflected. Paul's midrash on the desert-wandering in 1 Cor 10 is significant here.[143] In it, the idolatry of Israel in the wilderness is related specifically to the episode in question with a direct quotation (v. 7). Otherwise it is sufficient simply to refer to Acts 7:39-43.

The clear terminological reference to the Song of Moses - with the implications it had in early Judaism - in combination with the context of the event described by the Synoptics, appears as an indication of an associative connection with that which is narrated in Ex 32. The lines drawn to the first exodus in this case put special focus on the substantial manifestation of the lack of faith that the incident of the calf-worship below the mountain constituted (cf. below p. 53).[144]

This can open a further perspective. Anchored in the Old Testament prophecies there was a steady hope in early Judaism that in the future age of salvation, illness, suffering and want would no longer exist (cf.

---

195).

[141] אותו מעשה, meaning 'that unnameable deed'; *Num. Rab.* 5:3 (16b).

[142] Cf. *Midr. Ps.* 26 § 4 (109a), where Ps 26:5 ("I hate the assembly of evil-doers") is applied to the people who gathered themselves unto Aaron at the making of the molten calf (Ex 32:1).

[143] Cf. below chap. 10a.

[144] Cf. J. Guillet, "'Cette génération infidèle et dévoyée'", *RSR* 35, 1948, 279; D. Tabachovitz, *op. cit.*, 113 f.; J. Bowman, *The Gospel of Mark. The New Christian Jewish Passover Haggadah*, 1965, 199; G.M. de Tillesse, *Le secret messianique dans l' Evangile de Marc*, 1968, 98.

Jub. 23:26-30; *1 Enoch* 5:8 f.; 4 Ezra 8:52 ff.[145]). That influenced the picture of the wandering in the wilderness as a prototype for the era of eschatological fulfilment.[146] Within the scope of that theme a characteristic of the early Jewish view of the incident of the calf may have some interest in this connection. It is the recurrent thought - presumably existent already in primitive Christian times[147] - that people at the first exodus, in connection with the events at mount Sinai, had been liberated from such afflictions. In *Mek.* Ex 20:18 it is expressed in the following way (cf. Is 35:5[148]):

> When "they all stood before mount Sinai to receive the Torah there were - so Scripture tells us - no blind ones among them. For it is said: 'And the people saw'. It also tells that there were no dumb ones among them. For it is said: 'And all the people answered together' (Ex 19:8). And it also teaches that there were no deaf ones among them. For it is said: 'All that the Lord has spoken will we do and listen to' (Ex 24:7). And it also teaches that there were no lame ones among them. For it is said: 'And they stood at the nether part of the mount' (Ex 19:17). And it also teaches that there were no fools among them. For it is said: 'You have been shown to understand' (Deut 4:35)."

Even death is said to have lost its rule over the people. In a statement attributed to R. Jose (c. 150) it says: "It was upon this condition that the Israelites stood up before mount Sinai, on condition that the Angel of Death should have no power over them, for it is said: 'I said, You are godlike beings,' etc. (Ps 82:6)."[149] That, as well as other good things[150], was thus a blessing that the people received at Sinai. It was a manifestation that Israel belonged to God and was to live under his rule and bear its stamp. That ideal state was in turn seen as a typological prototype for the time of the eschatological salvation.[151]

However, that situation came to an end when the golden calf was made and the people worshipped it with sacrifice and singing and

---

[145] Further references in Str-B 1, 593 f.

[146] Cf. W. Wiebe, *Die Wüstenzeit als Typus der messianischen Heilszeit* (typed), 1939, 87.

[147] Cf. W. Wiebe, *op. cit.*, 88.

[148] In e.g. *Pesiqta* (ed. Buber) 55a; 106b–107a there is a clearly expressed parallel between different aspects of the Israelites' salvation at Sinai and that which is promised for the eschatological future in Is 35:5 f.; cf. Mt 11:4 f. However, the documentation here is late.

[149] *Mek.* Ex 20:19. For further references see Str-B 1, 594-596.

[150] Cf. W. Wiebe, *op. cit.*, 87 f.

[151] It can occur that Israel at Sinai is mentioned as a sort of sample (דגמה) of the world to come (*Pesiqta* [ed. Buber] 107a).

dancing (Ex 32:1 ff.). "When they committed that crime of calf-worship, their blemishes returned to them".[152] Then they also lost their supremacy over the Angel of Death.[153] The crime of the bull-calf was a 'Fall', which is sometimes placed side by side with that of Adam.[154]

If - as is probable - such thoughts were part of the contemporary Jewish frame of reference, it has not been without relevance as regards the view of Jesus' deeds and message.[155] The salvation gifts that were then thought of as having been lost at the incident of the calf below mount Sinai, are given through Jesus in the perspective of fulfilment. The prophetic promises for the future that, in the coming time of salvation, people would be liberated from illness and suffering (Is 29:18 f.; 35:5 f.; et al.), are being fulfilled through him.[156] That is emphasized in his answer to the question posed by the disciples of John earlier in Mt and Lk (Mt 11:2-6 par. Lk 7:18-23).

In this context, what happens up on the mountain is important. Jesus' transfiguration is a revelation scene, where Jesus appears in a glorified form, conversing with Moses and Elijah (Mk 9:2-8 par. Mt 17:1-8; Lk 9:28-36). The highlight is the heavenly voice proclaming Jesus as God's son[157] with the imperative: 'Listen to him' (ἀκούετε αὐτοῦ, in Lk in inverted order with the stress on the pronoun) - this exortation apparently relates to the saying about the coming prophet in Deut 18:15: 'Him shall you listen to' (LXX: αὐτοῦ ἀκούσεσθε).

According to the usual outlook in the New Testament, illness - physical or mental - is seen as the work of evil spirits. That is reflected in the formulation in Acts 10:38: Jesus went about "healing all that were opressed by the devil".[158] In his position as God's son victory over them

---

[152] *Num. Rab.* 7:1 (19b); further references in Str-B 1, 595 f. Cf. L. Ginzberg, *The Legends of the Jews* III, 119 ff.; 213.

[153] See e.g. L. Ginzberg, *op. cit.,* 120.

[154] Cf. F. Weber, *System der Altsynagogalen Palästinischen Theologie aus Targum, Midrasch und Talmud,* 1880, 262 ff.

[155] On this perspective cf. G. Friedrich, προφήτης κτλ., *TWNT* 6, 848: When Jesus in Mt 11:4 f. par. Lk 7:22 answers John the Baptist's question as he does "gibt er damit zu verstehen, dass er der messianische Prophet ist, der die paradiesischen Zustände der Wüstenzeit herbeiführt", which according to rabbinical opinions lasted "bis zur Anbetung des Kalbes". Cf. W. Wiebe, *op. cit.,* 116 f.; F. Hahn, *Christologische Hoheitstitel,* 2. Aufl. 1964, 393.

[156] Cf. above p. 38–39.

[157] Here the proclamation of the heavenly voice at the baptism of Jesus returns (Mk 1:11 par. Mt 3:17, Lk 3:22).

[158] B. Noack, *Satanás und Sotería,* 1948, 66 f.; H. Schlier, *Mächte und Gewalten im Neuen Testament,* 1958, 20 f.; O. Böcher, *Das Neue Testament und die dämonischen*

was given to him. At their meetings with Jesus, the demons revealed him as God's son (Lk 4:41; Mk 3:11; Mk 5:7 par. Mt 8:29; Lk 8:28) or the Holy One of God (Mk 1:24 par. Lk 4:34), and they trembled and fell down before him, and he cast them out. As God's son he had power over them. His victorious battle against them is evidence of the in-breaking kingdom of God (Mt 12:25-29 par.).[159]

When Jesus is proclaimed God's son by the heavenly voice on the mountain, it is implied, against this background, that he is the one who can defeat the evil spirits and free people from their rule and give the fruits of salvation as is prophesied in e.g. Is 35:5 f. (Mt 11:4 f. et al.).[160]

Below the mountain, however, it is demonstrated that those who have experienced his arrival and his deeds have not received in faith those gifts of liberation. The helpless crowd with the sick boy whom the disciples cannot heal is a manifestation of that. Note that in all the Gospels the illness is identified as possession by an evil spirit.[161] It is traced to a demon or an unclean spirit which has to be driven out (Mk 9:17-29; Mt 17:18 f.; Lk 9:39-42).

When Jesus begins to speak in this context he does it with the words: ὦ γενεὰ ἄπιστος (καὶ διεστραμμένη). How is this to be understood? To whom does it apply here? The failing disciples (primarily)?[162] Or both the disciples and the others?[163] Or Israel as a people?[164] The exodus typological orientation is indicated, as has become apparent above, already through the terminology. The *genea* conception has undoubtedly the same content as in the phrase 'this *genea*'. The aspect is salvation-historical. Characteristic of the *genea* is then that they have not accepted the gifts of salvation through Jesus at the second exodus, here concretely manifested in the event with the epileptic boy, where

Mächte, 1972, 19–21; and others.

[159] See further E. Lövestam, *Son and Saviour* (ConNT18), 1961, 101–103.

[160] Cf. F. Bovon, *Das Evangelium nach Lukas*, 1989, p. 512: "Durch den Sieg über den bösen Geist (9,37–43a) bestätigt sich die Beziehung Jesu zu Gott und seine heilende Kraft, deren Ursprung die Verklärung (9,28–36) blitzartig beleuchtet hat".

[161] For a treatment of Mk's version from this aspect see H. Riesenfeld, "De fientliga andarna. (Mk 9:14–29)", *SEÅ* 22–23, 1958, 64–74. Cf. R. Pesch, *Das Markusevangelium* II, 1977, 88.

[162] E.g. H.J. Held in G. Bornkamm-G. Barth-H.J. Held, *Überlieferung und Auslegung im Matthäusevangelium*, 4. Aufl., 1965, 181; H. Schürmann, *Das Lukasevangelium* I, 1969, 570; E.E. Ellis, *The Gospel of Luke*, 1974 (1983), 144.

[163] E.g. I.H. Marshall, *The Gospel of Luke*, 1978, 391; J. Fitzmyer, *The Gospel according to Luke* I, 1981, 809; C.F. Evans, *Saint Luke*, 1990, 423; W.D. Davies-D.C. Allison, *op. cit.*, 724.

[164] E.g. H. Frankemölle, *op. cit.*, 23 f.; U. Luz, *op. cit.*, 522.

several of the disciples are also involved[165]. From this perspective Jesus speaks in a generalizing fashion about the *genea*.[166]

As for the failing disciples it is apparent that in their case it is a matter of a lack of faith.[167] It is not suggested that they doubted Jesus' power to drive out the evil spirit and thus cure the sick boy - cf. in contrast the comment of the boy's father to Jesus: "If you can"... (Mk 9:22 f.). But the disciples, who according to Mt 10:1 (par. Lk 9:1; Mk 6:7) had been given authority (ἐξουσία) by Jesus over unclean spirits, to cast them out and to heal every disease, could not. When Mt in this context particularly mentions their lack of faith, he does not use the word 'unbelief' – as Mk does about the father ("I believe; help my ἀπιστία", v. 24) – but 'little belief' (ὀλιγοπιστία), the same expression which he uses to refer to them in several other places (ὀλιγόπιστος, Mt 8:26; 14:31; 16:8; cf. Mt 6:30; Lk 12:28).[168] Because of their little faith they could not cast the demon out (Mt 17:19 f.). When Jesus in Mk says that "this kind cannot be driven out by anything but prayer" (Mk 9:29), it has rightly been pointed out that prayer here does not involve a special technique but is closely connected to faith.[169] It has also been pointed out that within the story the disciples do not seem to apply Jesus' outburst principally to themselves, as they ask about the reasons for their own particular failure to drive out the demon (Mk 9:28 f.; Mt 17:19 f.).[170]

The generalizing *genea* passage with its contextual continuation (see below) apparently has as its function to be a serious warning even to the

---

[165] Note the hardly commendable role of Aaron at the incident of the golden calf (Ex 32).

[166] The *dor/genea* phrases in Deut 32:5,20, which Jesus' expression alludes to, have also a general form, notwithstanding there being people of another spirit (p. 15 f.).

[167] In Luke the healing activity of the disciples and the need for faith in that connection is not dealt with more closely. There "all the stress falls on the authority of Jesus himself" (I.H. Marshall, *The Gospel of Luke*, 1978, 389).

[168] Cf. H. Frankemölle, *Jahwebund und Kirche Christi*, 1974 (1984), 23; J. Gnilka, *Das Matthäusevangelium* II, 1988, 108 f.; U. Luz, *Das Evangelium nach Matthäus* II, 1990, 522-524 ("Kleinglaube ist wie 6,30; 8,26; 14,31; 16,8 mutlos gewordener Glaube und mangelndes Zutrauen in Gottes wunderbare Hilfe", p. 523); W.D. Davies-D.C. Allison, *The Gospel according to Saint Matthew* II, 1991, 727 ("Perhaps we should postulate behind Matthew two competing notions of faith - the one being saving faith /whose antithesis is unbelief/, the other the special faith required to perform great miracles... If so, the disciples have the former but not the latter").

[169] Cf. C.E.B. Cranfield, *The Gospel according to Saint Mark*, 1959, 305; Ch. D. Marshall, *Faith as a Theme in Mark's Narrative*, 1989, 222.

[170] Ch. D. Marshall, *op. cit.*, 117.

disciples with their ὀλιγοπιστία against walking in the counsel of the faithless *genea* (cf. Ps 1:1 and above p. 15 n. 43). At the same time Jesus' words about the power of faith (Mt 17:20; Mk 9:23) and his driving out of the demon and healing of the boy are a strong encouragement for them to believe in him wholeheartedly and receive the entire riches of salvation.[171]

At the experience of the unbelieving (and perverse) *genea* below the mountain Jesus asks (in Mk's formulation): ἕως πότε πρὸς ὑμᾶς (Mt: μεθ' ὑμῶν[172]) ἔσομαι; ἕως πότε ἀνέξομαι ὑμῶν; (Mk 9:19 par. Mt 17:17; Lk 9:41: ἕως πότε ἔσομαι πρὸς ὑμᾶς καὶ ἀνέξομαι ὑμῶν;). Stylistically there is a similar repetition of 'how long' (ἕως πότε, ἕως τίνος) in several texts in the LXX (e.g. LXX Ps 12:2 f.; 93:3; LXX Jer 29:5 f.).[173] In this case there may be reason to draw attention to some passages in Num 14, which are about the *dor* of the Wilderness, a theme that has been seen to lie in the background here.[174] After the spies' report about the promised land, we are told that the people in the desert oppose going there and wish instead to go back to Egypt (Num 14:1 ff.). Then the Lord says to Moses: "How long (ἕως τίνος) will this people despise me? And how long (ἕως τίνος) will they not believe in me, in spite of all the signs which I have wrought among them?" (v. 11). Further on in this chapter he asks in the same way: "How long (ἕως τίνος) shall this wicked congregation murmur against me?" (v. 27).

In Jesus' double-question it is, however, not a matter of how long the *genea* would despise and reject Jesus. It is rather how long he was to bear with it. That which primarily comes into focus is then the idea in ancient Israel that God reacted to the evil in a *dor* or a collective by hiding his face from it and abandoning it (cf. Deut 31:17; Acts 7:41 f.). This way of viewing matters is to be found precisely in the Song of Moses[175], where it is written: "'I will hide my face from them,' he said;

---

[171] Cf. H J. Held's comment that the final clause in Mt ("...nothing will be impossible to you", v. 20c) shows what the purpose of the entire passage is: "Es ist die Belehrung, wie die Jünger ihr Versagen überwinden" (*op. cit.*, 179).

[172] As to the Emmanuel/God-with-us perspective in this context in Mt see H. Frankemölle, *Jahwebund und Kirche Christi*, 1974, 21 ff.; 25-27; cf. J. Gnilka, *Das Matthäusevangelium* II, 1988, 104; 107; 109 f.; U. Luz, *Das Evangelium nach Matthäus* II, 1990, 522 f.

[173] E.g. H. Frankemölle, *op. cit.*, 24 f.; R. Pesch, *Das Markusevangelium* II, 1977, 90.

[174] Cf. D. Tabachovitz, *Die Septuaginta und das Neue Testament*, 1956, 114 f.; J. Gnilka, *op.cit.*, 107.

[175] Cf. above p. 25 f.

'let me see what their end will be, for they are a perverse *dor* (דּוֹר תַּהְפֻּכֹת)'..." (Deut 32:20). That God here is said to hide his face from them, is sometimes expressed in the rabbinic literature by saying that he removes his Shekinah. Thus in *Tg. Onq.* ad loc.: "I will take away my Shekinah from amongst them". Likewise e.g. in *Sipre Deut.* (§ 320 [137a]).[176] Besides v. 5 it is precisely this passage in Deut 32 - v. 20 - to which the formulation γενεὰ ἄπιστος (καὶ διεστραμμένη) in Jesus' address to those gathered below the mountain associates.[177] There can then be no doubt that it has to be seen against that background when Jesus asks: "How long am I to be with you? How long am I to bear with you?" (Mt 17:17 par.). He expresses himself in a way and with a form which brings to the fore the idea of the the divine Presence's withdrawal from the *dor* of the Wilderness.

In this light Jesus' question is given its significant meaning. In the gospel pericope, as otherwise in the Synoptics, it is Jesus, to whom the *genea* are related. The salvation-historical situation with the gifts of radical liberation is dependent on him, his mission and his deeds. If he leaves the *genea*, it is equivalent to God withdrawing his redeeming Presence with an eschatalogical calamity as a result.

The text has thus something substantial to say about Jesus and his *exousia*. His words may be said to imply that he is from another world and will return there. But what we find in the pericope is not the mythical motif of God, "der nur vorübergehend in Menschengestalt erschien, um alsbald in den Himmel zurückzukehren".[178] Jesus is 'the second Redeemer' in the sense of the fulfilment of the Scriptures. And when he complainingly warns the *genea*, who do not accept the gifts, it is done through an application in the *first person* of a mode of expression that the Lord himself uses in his words of judgement on the *dor* of the Wilderness in Deut 32, an implicit expression that it is the presence of God that is to be found in him.[179]

---

[176] Cf. how God's Shekinah is also said to have been taken from the *dor* of the Flood, e.g. in *3 Enoch* 48 C:1: "When I beheld the men of the *dor* of the Flood, that they were corrupt, then I went and removed my Shekinah from among them".

[177] Above p. 47.

[178] R. Bultmann quoting M. Dibelius (*Die Geschichte der synoptischen Tradition*, 7. Aufl., 1967, 169).

[179] NB the basic question of the people in the wilderness in Ex 17:7: "Is the Lord among us or not?"

6. The eschatological Sayings in Mk 8:38 and Lk 17:22-37

a) *Mark 8:38*

In Mk 8:34 ff. there are a number of *logia* dealing with discipleship (following Jesus' first prediction of his passion in vs. 31–33). There is also a *genea*-saying in v. 38. It runs: "If anyone is ashamed of me and my words[180] in this adulterous and sinful *genea* (ἐν τῇ γενεᾷ ταύτῃ τῇ μοιχαλίδι καὶ ἁμαρτωλῷ), the Son of Man will be ashamed of him, when he comes in the glory of his Father and of the holy angels". In par. Lk 9:26 the phrase 'in this adulterous and sinful *genea*' is missing, and in the corresponding *logia* in Lk 12:9 par. Mt 10:33 it says instead 'before men' (ἐνώπιον τῶν ἀνθρώπων and ἔμπροσθεν τῶν ἀνθρώπων respectively).

Against ἐν τῇ γενεᾷ ταύτῃ... in the Markan *logion* is contrasted - with the Son of Man as the subject - ὅταν ἔλθῃ ἐν τῇ δόξῃ τοῦ πατρὸς αὐτοῦ... The latter formulation apparently refers to Dan 7:13 f., and it can scarcely be anything other than the *parousia* that is meant.[181] Ἡ γενεὰ αὕτη is thus that *genea* that will last until the return of the Son of Man. C.E.B. Cranfield finds the phrase ἐν τῇ γενεᾷ ταύτῃ here to be roughly equivalent to ἐν τῷ καιρῷ τούτῳ in 10:30, which is contrasted with ἐν τῷ αἰῶνι τῷ ἐρχομένῳ.[182] At the same time he emphasizes that the *genea* is not thought of simply as a period of time, but the thought of the men living in it and of their character is also present and prominent.[183] This is apparent from the accompanying qualifications. The adjectives used to characterize 'this *genea*' are μοιχαλίς, 'adulterous', and ἁμαρτωλός, 'sinful'. Cf. Mt

---

[180] In P45vid W k sa λόγους is missing. If this is the original reading, then it stands: "If anyone is ashamed of me and mine..." The text used here, however, has better authentication.

[181] Cf. W.G. Kümmel, "Das Verhalten Jesus gegenüber und das Verhalten des Menschensohns. Markus 8,38 par und Lukas 12,3 f par Matthäus 10,32 f', *Jesus und der Menshensohn* (FS A. Vögtle), 1975, 218, 220; R. Pesch, *Das Markusevangelium* II, 1977, 64 f.; M. Müller, *Der Ausdruck 'Menschensohn' in den Evangelien*, 1984, 101–103.

[182] Cf. Lk 16:8:..."the children of this age/world (οἱ υἱοὶ τοῦ αἰῶνος τούτου) are more prudent in dealing with their own *genea* (τὴν γενεὰν τὴν ἑαυτῶν) than are the children of light".

[183] *The Gospel according to Saint Mark*, 1959, 284.

12:39 and 16:4: γενεὰ πονηρὰ καὶ μοιχαλίς.[184] In Mk it is, of course, a question of sin and faithlessness towards the Lord manifested in a denial of Jesus, with attacks on him and those who believe in him. The phrase thus fits into the use of the *dor/genea* terminology in other synoptic texts documented above and receives its significance in that light.

In the *logion* the behaviour of the believers in the Son of Man is put in relation to 'this *genea*'. It is expected to be at variance with the *dor/genea*, which agrees well with ancient Jewish conceptions.[185] Such a contrasting situation can be seen from different perspectives, something which can be illustrated by the following rabbinic reasoning.

In Gen 7:1 the Lord says to Noah: "I have found you righteous before me in this *dor* (בדור הזה, LXX: ἐν τῇ γενεᾷ ταύτῃ)" (cf. Gen 6:9). By reason of this formulation the rabbis can discuss whether Noah was righteous in an unconditional sense or merely in comparison with the *dor* of the Flood. In *Gen. Rab.* 30:9 (63a) e.g. this line of reasoning is followed by R. Judah and R. Nehemiah (c. 150 AD). The former states: "Only in his generations was he a righteous man (by comparison); had he flourished in the generation of Moses or in the generation of Samuel, he would not have been called righteous: in the street of the totally blind, the one-eyed man is called clear-sighted, and the infant is called a scholar". R. Judah thus means that Noah was judged in comparison with his ungodly contemporaries and, seen against that dark background, found to be righteous.[186] R. Nehemiah sees the matter from another perspective when he states: "If he (Noah) was righteous even in his own generations (*scil.* in spite of his corrupt environment), how much more (had he lived) in the generation of Moses or in the generation of Samuel".[187] In spite of the greater difficulties of living according to God's will in a sinful *dor*, where the righteous could be despised, jeered at and persecuted, Noah remained constant. That is R. Nehemiah's argument. The *dor/genea* functions in a corresponding manner in Mk as in Noah's case. The basic assumption is the same as in

---

[184] Regarding μοιχαλίς as a term for severe faithlessness to God, see above p. 36. As for ἁμαρτωλός see K.H. Rengstorf, ἁμαρτωλός κτλ., *TWNT* 1, 320-337.

[185] Cf. above chap. 1.

[186] M. G. Steinhauser sees the passage about the dishonest manager in Lk 16:8 from this perspective: he "becomes a model but with the qualification 'in his own generation'"; "Noah in his Generation: An Allusion in Luke 16,8b, 'εἰς τὴν γενεὰν τὴν ἑαυτῶν'", *ZNW* 79, 1988, 152-157.

[187] The same reasoning is found e.g. in *b. Sanh.* 108a, there attributed to R. Jochanan and Resh Lakish.

R. Nehemiah but it has another application.

It is the demands for wholeheartedness and radicalism in the disciples which are developed in Mk 8:34-37, that are followed up in v. 38 by the *logion* of what will happen at the glorious advent of the Son of Man. It is done with the use of the verb ἐπαισχύνεσθαι, 'be ashamed of': "If anyone is ashamed of me ..., the Son of Man will be ashamed of him ..."[188] As noted above this saying occurs in a parallel or corresponding form in other places in the Synoptics (Lk 9:26 and Mt 10:33/Lk 12:9 respectively).[189] That shows how important it was for the early Christian congregation.[190] When Mark in this connection has the ἡ γενεὰ αὕτη-formulation in question, what does it imply?

It has been seen above that according to the early Jewish conception living in an evil *dor/genea* had consequences for anyone who was 'of another spirit'. It has also become clear that this did not only mean living in generally unpleasant surroundings but that the unpleasantness also included actions carried out by the *dor/genea*.[191] Anyone who distanced himself from the godless attitude of the *dor/genea* had to be ready to be subjected to trials of different kinds. The situation thus implied temptations to give in and adapt. Within the framework of the conception in question the character of temptation is clearly marked in e.g. 2 Pet 2:9 (regarding Lot and the people of Sodom): "The Lord

---

[188] Mark clearly identifies Jesus with the Son of Man.

[189] The saying in its substance can apparently be traced to Jesus; see e.g. E. Percy, *Die Botschaft Jesu*, 1953, 249 f.; J. Gnilka, *Das Evangelium nach Markus* II, 1979, 27; J. Coppens, "Les logia du Fils de l'homme dans l'évangile de Marc", *L'Evangile selon Marc* (BETL 34), 1988, 504; cf. R. Bultmann, *Die Geschichte der synoptischen Tradition*, 7. Aufl. 1967, 163. It plays an essential role as regards the question of the Son of Man, which, however, will not be dealt with more closely here. Concerning the priority of the different versions of the saying, most scholars place Mk 8:38 before par. Lk 9:26. Lk 12:9 / Mt 10:33 are normally put ahead of the Markan version - if we are not dealing with two different sayings, which some scholars assume as possible (e.g. C.E.B. Cranfield, *op. cit.*, 283). However, cf. M. Hooker who finds that her "examination of the way in which the eschatalogical sayings are employed by the three Synoptic evangelists suggests that Matthew and Luke reflect a later stage in the development of the concept of the Son of man than does Mark" ("The Son of Man and the Synoptic Problem", *The Four Gospels 1992* [BETL 100], 1992, 199). Regarding the presence of the phrase 'this adulterous and sinful *genea*' in Mk, it can be observed *that* it cannot be shown to be Markan (cf. W.G. Kümmel, *op. cit.*, 216), *that* the *dor/genea* concept in question was firmly anchored in the ancient Jewish world of ideas, *that* the special use of it in Mk 8:38 has, *mutatis mutandis*, a corresponding use in rabbinical literature, and *that* the phrase according to New Testament witnesses was characteristic of Jesus' way of expressing himself.

[190] Cf. E. Haenchen, *Der Weg Jesu*, 1966, 298.

[191] See above chap. 4.

knows how to rescue the goodly ἐκ πειρασμοῦ".[192]

The phrase ἐν τῇ γενεᾷ ταύτῃ τῇ μοιχαλίδι καὶ ἁμαρτωλῷ in Mk 8:38 indicates in this way that the disciples are in a continual state of temptation. It demands a wholehearted devotion under such circumstances to hold fast to a faith in Jesus and not be ashamed of him. But that is the gift and vocation of being a disciple. As giving way in this matter and adjusting to 'this *genea*' and not being prepared to share in Jesus' shame and suffering, means not being acknowledged by the Son of Man at his advent in glory but sharing with the *genea* in the coming judgement.

The phrase in question thus emphasizes the conditions which distinguish the existential situation of the believers up until the glorious eschatological coming of the Son of Man. It is a question of temptation and risk (cf. Mt 23:34-36 with par.). Its function is not, of course, only to be a sober piece of information about a factual situation. It has the character of a call to action. The words 'in this adulterous and sinful *genea*' are a signal with a significant content in the New Testament context regarding the conditions of being a disciple.

b) *Luke 17:22-37*

Apart from the eschatalogical discourse in Lk 21:5 ff., which is in all essentials par. to Mk 13:1 ff., the Gospel according to Luke has an eschatalogical section in chapter 17:22 ff. Its contents are to a large extent parallel to those in Mt 24[193] but only to a small extent parallel to Mk 13.[194]

There Jesus addresses his disciples and teaches them about the eschatalogical future. The coming of the Son of Man will happen suddenly and be clearly observable by all. But first - it is stressed - he must endure much suffering and be rejected by 'this *genea*' (v. 25). In the continuation it says that the condition in which the people will be on the day when the Son of Man is revealed, will be just as it was in the days of Noah when the Flood came, and in the days of Lot when Sodom was struck by the judgement of God. In vs. 31-35 further admonitions regarding 'that day' are given, and v. 37 adds a saying as an answer to

---

[192] Cf Lk 8:13b and E. Fuchs & P. Reymond, *La deuxième épitre de Saint Pierre. L'épitre de Saint Jude*, 1980, 87.

[193] The teaching is closely parallel to Mt 24:23 (or 26), 27, 28, 37–39, 17 f., 40 f.

[194] Cf. D. Lührmann, *Die Redaktion der Logienquelle*, 1969, 71–75.

the disciples' question, 'where?'.

The disciples' difficult situation in the future is in focus. It is clearly expressed when Jesus says to them in v. 22 that the time will come when they will long to see one of the days of the Son of Man, but they will not see it.

There has been much discussion as to what is meant here by 'one of the days of the Son of Man'. Different interpretations have been suggested. Does the phrase refer to the period inaugurated by the *parousia*, so that what the disciples long for is to see a day of the Son of Man's rule? Or to its first day, i.e. the day of the *parousia* itself? Or does it refer to the period between Easter and the *parousia*, when Jesus is exalted but hidden from the disciples, who long for his revelation? Or to the earthly days of the Son of Man? Or to the various glorious manifestations of the Son of Man at the transfiguration, resurrection, ascension and on other occasions?[195] Now it is obvious that - as R. Schnackenburg puts it - "Der ganze Horizont ist ein eschatologischer"[196]. A futural interpretation therefore would appear most likely. There would, however, hardly be sufficient grounds for interpreting 'one' (μίαν, i.e. one of the days....) as equivalent to 'first', referring to the *parousia*. What the disciples will desire to see appears then to be one of the coming days of the Son of Man when he will manifest himself as Victor and Saviour.[197]

This longing of the disciples will, however, not be fulfilled. In that context they are warned by Jesus against listening to people who say to them, "Look, there it is; or here it is". When the day has come, the

---

[195] See e.g. J. Zmijewski, *Die Eschatologiereden des Lukas-Evangeliums*, 1972, 400-403; I.H. Marshall, *The Gospel of Luke*, 1978, 658 f.; J. Fitzmyer, *The Gospel According to Luke* II, 1985, 1168 f. (all with ref.).

[196] "Der eschatologische Abschnitt Lk 17,20–37", *Mélanges bibliques* (FS B. Rigaux), 1970, 228.

[197] In vs. 26 ff. the phrase ('the days of the Son of Man') corresponds to 'the days of Noah' and 'the days of Lot'. It must, however, be observed that 'the days of Noah' did not end at the Flood, nor did 'the days of Lot' end with the destruction of Sodom. This is also expressed in the text; see vs. 27, 29: Noah and Lot lived on. 'The days' of Noah, of Lot is a more comprehensive way of expression which can include within its framework 'the day' that Noah went into the ark (v. 27), 'the day' that Lot went out from Sodom (v. 29). In a similar way regarding 'the days of the Son of Man'; within this framework you can find mentioned 'his day' (v. 24: ἐν τῇ ἡμέρᾳ αὐτοῦ, a phrase which is, however, omitted in important mss) and 'the day' when he is revealed (v. 30). That which is specifically meant when it refers to the days of Noah and Lot respectively in vs. 26 ff. and correspondingly to 'the days of the Son of Man' there is clear enough, but then due to the context (cf. Mt 24:37-39). In a corresponding fashion the context definitely indicates a futural reference in the phrase 'the days of the Son of Man' in v. 22.

arrival of the Son of Man will be manifest to all, like the lightning-flash that lights up the earth from end to end (vs. 23 f.).

This is where the saying : "But first he must suffer many things and be repudiated ἀπὸ τῆς γενεᾶς ταύτης" (v. 25) comes in. These words of Jesus agree in all essentials with Jesus' first announcement of his passion in Lk 9:22 (par. Mk 8:31; Mt 16:21). There, however, those who are acting against Jesus are described as 'the elders and chief priests and scribes', while Lk has 'this *genea*'.[198]

As has been noted 'this *genea*' is followed immediately by a comparison with the situation when the Flood came and when Sodom was destroyed (vs. 26 ff.). It is thus 'the *dor* of the Flood' and 'the men of Sodom' it refers to. It is then quite clear that the phrase ἡ γενεὰ αὕτη here comes within the framework of the *dor/genea* terminology in early Judaism and the New Testament discussed above. In several gospel texts the term has been shown to refer to 'the *dor* of the Wilderness'. In Lk 17, it is, however, the *parousia* and the eschatological salvation and judgement that belong with it that are in focus. Then it is the situation at 'the first end' of the world which is typologically emphasized as well as the situation at the destruction of Sodom.[199] This is also the case in Mt 24:34-39 (see below chap. 8), where there is, however, no reference to the Sodomites. It is hard to say if the reference to the people of Sodom can have been removed by Mt[200] or if it can have been added by Lk[201]. Whatever the case may be it plays an important role in Luke's

---

[198] Most scholars mean that in v. 25 it is a case of an editorial Lukan insertion, while others maintain a positive attitude to the matter of authenticity, e.g. T.W. Manson, *The Sayings of Jesus*, 1971, 142 f.; W.G. Kümmel, *Die Theologie des Neuen Testaments*, 1969, 79 f.; cf. J. Roloff, "Anfänge der soteriologischen Deutung des Todes Jesu (Mk. X. 45 und Lk. XXII. 27)", *NTS* 19, 1972, 40 n. 1; I.H. Marshall, *The Gospel of Luke*, 1978, 661 f. Regarding the term 'this *genea*' in the Lukan passage W. Michaelis' reasoning does not lack weight when he argues against the opinion that the phrase might be a secondary summary of the named instances in Lk 9:22: "Eher ist jedoch umgekehrt die Aufzählung der Instanzen 9,22 Par eine sekundäre Erweiterung auf Grund des tatsächlichen Anteils des Hohen Rats am geschichtlichen Ablauf der Ereignisse" (πάσχω κτλ.,*TWNT* 5, 913 n. 78).

[199] It often happens in ancient Jewish literature that these historical examples are combined; see Wis 10:4, 6; Sir 16:7 f.; 3 Macc 2:4 f.; *Jub* 20:5; *T. Napht.* 3:4 f.; Philo, *De vita Mos.* II,10 § 52-56; *Mek.* Ex 14:21; 15:6; *Sipre Deut.* 311 (134a); 318 (136a); *Gen. Rab.* 27:3 (59a); *Lev. Rab.* 23:9 (33b), etc.; cf. above p.11. Likewise in the Samaritan *Memar Marqah* IV § 5, § 12; VI § 2. Cf. 2 Pet 2:5-8. – Regarding the Sodom and Gomorrah theme in the Old Testament, early Jewish and early Christian traditions see J.A. Loader, *A Tale of Two Cities*, 1990.

[200] E.g. I.H. Marshall, *The Gospel of Luke*, 1978, 662 (with ref.).

[201] E.g. C.F. Evans, *Saint Luke*, 1990, 632.

text.[202]

That the righteous in a godless and wicked *dor/genea* were subjected to trials and dangers was an integral part of the conditions, as has been seen above. In the passage in Lk it is then Noah and Lot who are implicitly brought to the fore by the context.[203] According to Josephus, for instance, Noah was afraid that he would be killed, and therefore he departed out of the land.[204] In *Lev. Rab.* 27:5 (39b) it is said that Noah was pursued by his *dor*, etc.[205] Due mainly to the event described in Gen 19:30-38, Lot appears in many rabbinical sayings as a sinner, who can only be called righteous in comparison with his godless contemporaries.[206] There are, however, also texts which describe him as righteous in an unconditional sense, for example Wis 10:6: "When the ungodly perished, she (viz. Wisdom) delivered a righteous man, who fled from the fire that came down on the Five Cities".[207] This tradition is strongly marked e.g. in 2 Pet 2:7-8, where Lot's righteousness is stressed thrice: God "rescued *righteous* Lot, greatly distressed by the licentiousness of the wicked, for by what that *righteous* man saw and heard as he lived among them, he was vexed in his *righteous* soul day after day with their lawless deeds".[208] However Lot may have been regarded in different traditions, part of the picture of him was that he was attacked by those surrounding him (Gen 19:4 ff.). Lot had to suffer 'the men of Sodom', just as Noah suffered with 'the *dor* of the Flood'.

In a similar way to how God's messengers and righteous men throughout history have been challenged and attacked by sinful *dorot/geneai*, so also will the Son of Man be treated by 'this *genea*' before his revelation in glory.[209] In the context in Lk the function of the saying is a warning to the disciples not to expect his eschatalogocal manifestation until he has suffered and been rejected. In this there is

---

[202] See below.

[203] Cf. above p. 22 ff. regarding Moses.

[204] *Ant.* I,3:1 § 74.

[205] See further below p. 107.

[206] For references see Str-B 3, 769-771.

[207] Cf. *b. Ber.* 54b (Bar.). This excusing view of Lot in the perspective of Gen 19:30-38 is connected to the fact that king David - and thus also David's son, the Messiah - were descended from Lot and his daughters (via the Moabite, Ruth). See S. Rappaport, "Der gerechte Lot. Bemerkung zu II Ptr 2,7.8", *ZNW* 29, 1930, 299-304.

[208] Cf. *1 Clem.* 11:1.

[209] O. Cullmann rightly points out: Lk 17:25 "weist ... wohl nicht nur auf eine chronologische, sondern auch eine sachliche Vorbedingung des Endes" (*Heil als Geschichte*, 1965, 205 f.).

also a stressing of the *genea*'s character and a reminder of what the disciples themselves must be prepared to go through, in their Lord's footsteps (cf. chap. 6a).

With a view to his *parousia*, the *dor* of the Flood and the people of Sodom are given, in the continuation, as warning examples for the disciples (vs. 26 ff.) Both of them had made themselves known for unrighteousness and sin, and that is naturally assumed. But that is not focused in Jesus' saying. Instead what is stressed in both cases is the everyday, unworried existence of the people until the catastrophe strikes them (cf. Mt 24:37 ff.).[210] It is thus the unexpected and the surprising when the Son of Man 'is revealed' that this typological comparison is intended to stress – in agreement with the words about the lightning-flash in v. 24. From the use of both examples in early Jewish literature one can, however, assume that they are, at the same time, meant to mark the sure and unavoidable punishment of God on ungodly *dorot* and collectives.[211] Jesus' words then mean a striking exhortation to the disciples to live so that they are constantly ready for his revelation. To express it in a recurrent New Testament imagery: an exhortation not to fall asleep (through surrendering to the spirit of this world) but to be constantly awake while waiting for his arrival[212] – cf. how in e.g. Lk 21:34-36 it can even be 'cares of this life' that can make the hearts be weighed down, so that the day of revelation comes suddenly like a snare.[213]

The importance of the warning examples from the Old Testament in the account in Lk is underlined by the fact that also in the continuation it makes associations to the story of Sodom (vs. 31-33). In Gen 19 the angels told Lot, "Flee for your life; do not look back (μὴ περιβλέψῃς εἰς τὰ ὀπίσω)"... (v. 17); but Lot's wife looked back (ἐπέβλεψεν...εἰς τὰ ὀπίσω) and became as a pillar of salt (v. 26). Against this background the disciples are exorted, at the *parousia*, when 'this *genea*' is to be struck by the eschatalogical doom, not to have their minds on what has been but leave it and unconditionally accept salvation. The man who is on the roof must not come down to pick up his belongings; and likewise he who is in the field must not turn back (μὴ ἐπιστρεψάτω εἰς τὰ ὀπίσω) – and in that context specific reference is made to Lot's

---

[210] Neither in the case of the *dor* of the Flood or the men of Sodom is there mention of their special sins (cf. above p. 10 f. and Gen 19; Wis 10:7).

[211] See J. Schlosser, "Les jours de Noé et de Lot. A propos de *Luc*, XVII, 26-30", *RB* 80, 1973, 13-36.

[212] On this theme see E. Lövestam, *Spiritual Wakefulness in the New Testament*, 1963, passim.

[213] E. Lövestam, *op. cit.*, 122–133. Cf. in this connection Lk 8:14 par.

wife (vs. 31 f.).

Regarding the following saying in v. 33 ("Whoever tries to save his life will lose it, but whoever loses his life will preserve it"), there are different opinions about its tradition history and original context.[214] In the gospel traditions it marks the danger of being too oriented towards the present age and being tied by it; see Mk 8:35 f. par. Mt 16:25 f., Lk 9:24 f. (cf. Mt 10:39; Jn 12:25) – it is only in Jesus, the Son of Man, that eternal life can be found.[215] In its context in Lk 17 this saying too has apparently a special reference to the Sodom story, namely as an allusion to the words of the angel to Lot immediately before he is told not to look back in Gen 19:17: σῴζων σῷζε τὴν σεαυτοῦ ψυχήν.[216] Lot and his family were to save their lives by fleeing and not looking back, something which Lot's wife did not abide by, with tragic consequences. Thus shall Jesus' disciples on his arrival also be free from all ties to that which bears the mark of decay and dissolution and are doomed to go under (cf. Lk 21:33 with par.). The saying can in this way be seen as a summary of what is said in vs. 31-33.

In vs. 34-35 the radical separation at the *parousia* between those who will be saved and the others is emphasized, using the terms 'be taken' (παραλαμβάνεσθαι) and 'be left' (ἀφίεσθαι): two men will be in one bed, and one will be taken, and the other left; two women will be grinding at the same mill, and one will be taken and the other left. This expression is in complete agreement with the notions which were related to the Flood and the destruction of Sodom. For those people who were not struck down by the catastrophe, their salvation was due to the fact that they had escaped from the *dor* or collective that suffered God's punishment.[217] The terminology in question in Lk should be seen against this background. This is also supported by the fact that the parallel passage in Mt comes in connection with a typological comparison of that which is going to happen at the *parousia* with that which happened at the time of Noah (Mt 24:37-41). In this light there can be no doubt as to the answer to the question whether 'be taken' is to be understood in the

---

[214] Cf. J. Zmijewski, *op. cit.*, 479-482.

[215] In Jesus' saying in Lk 17:33 the phrase of giving one's life ἕνεκεν ἐμοῦ (Mk 8:35; Mt 10:39; 16:25; Lk 9:24) is missing. Cf. J. Zmijewski's explanation that the reason is, that "es ihm nicht mehr um die 'Aufforderung zur Martyriumsbereitschaft' geht, sondern um das Problem der 'Preisgabe des Irdischen', wie sie im Blick auf die Parusie des Menschensohnes verlangt wird" (*op. cit.*, 482, in connection with J. Schmid).

[216] Cf. L. Hartman, "Reading Luke 17,20–37", *The Four Gospels 1992* (FS F. Neirynck), 1992, 1668–1670.

[217] See above p. 12 ff.

negative sense of being taken for judgement or in the positive one of being saved. It is clearly a matter of the latter.[218]

In connection with Jesus' saying in vs. 34-35 (ἀποκριθέντες...) the disciples ask a question in v. 37: "Where (ποῦ), Lord?" There has been much discussion as to the meaning of this. What does the 'Where' refer to? The place for the coming of the Son of Man/the Judgement? Or the place to which those who are taken away are brought? Or where those who are left are to be found?[219] And what does Jesus' answer mean? The 'Where?' of the disciples comes immediately after ἀφεθήσεται: (the other) 'will be left'. If one bears that in mind and the question then applies to where those being left are going to be found[220], the notion of the Flood and the punishment of Sodom is in all probability also in the background here. Just as in early Judaism it is assumed that the *dor* of the Flood went under in their entirety, the same also applies to the men of Sodom.[221] It is also emphasized in the text: the catastrophe "destroyed them all (ἀπώλεσεν πάντας)" (vs. 27 and 29). In the New Testament we find the same total aspect regarding 'this *genea*' - for those who are not of a different spirit and thus become saved.[222] We apparently have to see and understand Jesus' answer from this perspective. He does not give a direct reply to the question 'Where?', but his proverbial saying implies that none who is left behind can avoid punishment. "Where the corpse is, there the vultures will gather"[223] - this is then a way of expressing the universality of God's judgement on ἡ γενεὰ αὕτη at 'the second end' of the world.

The account in Lk 17:22-37 has a decided eschatalogical approach. It is about the *parousia* and its consequences for mankind of different ways of life. In Jesus' teaching of his disciples in this case the typology of 'the *dor* of the Flood' and that of 'the people of Sodom' play a substantial part. With the use of them an impressive picture of the present spiritual situation and the eschatological future, at the coming of

---

[218] Cf. I.H. Marshall, *op. cit.*, 668; J. Fitzmyer, *op. cit.*, 1172. . When it says in *Jub.* 22:22: "Just as the sons of Sodom were taken from the earth, so (too) all of those who worship idols shall be taken away", it is said from the perspective given in the preceding sentence: ..."they will have no memory upon the earth".

[219] For different suggestions as to interpretation (with ref.) see J. Zmijewski, *Die Eschatologiereden des Lukas-Evangeliums*, 1972, 513–518.

[220] See e.g. W. Grundmann, *Das Evangelium nach Lukas*, 1961, 345; E. Haenchen, *Der Weg Jesu*, 1966, 457.

[221] E.g. Is 1:9; Josephus, *Ant.* I,11:4 § 202; *Memar Marqah* VI § 2.

[222] See e.g. chap. 9 below.

[223] This saying comes earlier in Mt 24, immediately following v. 27.

the Son of Man, is given. That has not only a cognitive bearing. The semantic function of the text is mainly admonitory[224], and the admonitory character is emphasized strongly by the very typological references to these entities, with their basis in the Old Testament and their firm place in the ancient Jewish world of ideas.

---

[224] See L. Hartman, *op. cit.*, 1675.

7. Judgement on ἡ γενεὰ αὕτη

Jesus' prophecy of judgement on ἡ γενεὰ αὕτη in Mt 23:34-36 par. Lk 11:49-51 is part of his sayings against the scribes and Pharisees (Mt; Lk: the Pharisees and the lawyers). After the pronouncement in question there is in Luke a final 'woe', while in Matthew it rounds off the 'woes' and is followed by the lament over Jerusalem[225].[226]

The presentation varies in the two Gospels, but in both of them 'this *genea*' is in focus. It is to be struck by the impending punishment.

In both cases reference is made in the context to the forebears' killing of the prophets and the addressees' building of their tombs. But the formulation differs to some extent.[227]

In Mt 23:29-33 Jesus thus pronounces his 'woe' over the scribes and Pharisees[228] who build up the tombs of the prophets and embellish the monuments of the righteous[229] and say, "If we had been alive in our fathers' time, we should never have taken part with them in shedding the blood of the prophets". By their acts and comments, they believe themselves to demonstrate a different attitude to that of their ancestors and thus disavowe the latter's malicious deeds. But in Jesus' saying it is taken as evidence that they are sons of those who killed the prophets - 'to be son of' here evidently implies kinship of character.[230] And they

---

[225] In Luke the lament over the city is found in another connexion (Lk 13:34 f.). Many scholars hold that Matthew has preserved the more original order (e.g. R. Bultmann, *Die Geschichte der synoptischen Tradition*, 7. Aufl. 1967, 120; S. Légasse, "L'oracle contre 'cette génération' [Mt 23,34-36 par. Lc 11,49-51]", *Logia. Les paroles de Jésus* [Mémorial J. Coppens], 1982, 237-239; H. Schürmann, "Die Redekomposition wider 'dieses Geschlecht'", *SNTU* Ser. A, Bd 11, 1986, 56-58), and the apostrophe of Jerusalem at least fits the context better in Mt than in Lk (cf. C.F. Evans, *Saint Luke*, 1990, 563).

[226] As for the questions of tradition and composition cf. H. Schürmann, *op. cit.*, 33–81 (with lit. ref.).

[227] Cf. I.H. Marshall, *The Gospel of Luke*, 1978, 500 f. (with ref.); C.E. Evans, *Saint Luke*, 1990, 507 f.

[228] As for the naming of them as 'hypocrites' cf. D. Garland, *The Intention of Matthew 23*, 1979, 104-117.

[229] Regarding the raising of grave monuments in old Palestine see especially J. Jeremias, *Heiligengräber in Jesu Umwelt*, 1958, 118–125. – For suggestions as to a word-play in this case see M. Black, *An Aramaic Approach to the Gospels and Acts*, 3rd ed., 1967, 12 f.; D. Derrett, "'You build the Tombs of the Prophets' (Lk. 11,47-51, Mt. 23,29-31)", *TU* 102, 1968, 187-193. - Cf. the placing together of 'prophet' and 'righteous man' in Mt 10:41.

are urged to fill up the measure of their fathers (v. 32).[231] This is an ironic imperative in the prophetic style; cf. Amos 4:4: "Come to Bethel and transgress"...[232] In the following verse those addressed by Jesus - as representatives of Israel's rebelliousness called 'serpents', 'offspring of vipers' - are then asked how they could escape the judgement of Gehenna (v. 33).

In Luke the saying is addressed to the lawyers (11:45 ff.).[233] Jesus says his 'woe' to them as they build the tombs of the prophets, whom their fathers murdered, and continues: "Thereby (ἄρα) you give testimony that you approve of the deeds of your fathers; they murdered the prophets, and you build (their tombs)" (v. 48). The building of the tombs of the prophets was of course done in order to honor their memory and thus distance themselves from their forbears' deeds against them, although this is not said directly here. And that was something other than to kill them. None the less both acts are somehow seen here as similar. As J. Fitzmyer puts it: "By building the tombs, association in the guilt of their forebears is manifested".[234]

It should be noted that when the misdeeds of the forefathers are discussed it is not unrighteousness in general that is spoken of. It is their treatment of the prophets (and - in Mt - the righteous). The fact that people in Israel pursued and killed God's prophets has grounds in the Old Testament (1 Kings 19:10,14; 2 Chron 24:20 f.; Neh 9:26; Jer 2:30; 26:20 ff.) and it seems to have been a generally held idea in the early Jewish and Christian period, seen in such texts as Mt 5:12, Acts 7:52 and 1 Thess 2:15.[235] It is such behaviour by the forefathers towards God's envoys to his people in the past that is referred to in Jesus' saying.

---

[230] Cf. P. Hoffmann, *Studien zur Theologie der Logienquelle*, 1972, 163 f.; I.H. Marshall, *The Gospel of Luke*, 1978, 501; D. Garland, *op. cit.,* 165 f. (with ref.).

[231] Both external and inner evidence indicates that the imperative reading should be preferred to the *var. lect.*

[232] Cf. J. Gnilka, *Das Matthäusvangelium* II, 1988, 296.

[233] Whereas Mt 23:13-36 has seven 'woes' directed consistently against the scribes and the Pharisees, Lk 11:42-52 has two sets of three 'woes' directed against the Pharisees and the lawyers respectively. Cf. J. Fitzmyer, *The Gospel according to Luke X-XXIV,* 1985, 943; H. Schürmann, "Die Redekomposition wider 'dieses Geschlecht'", *SNTU* Ser. A, Bd 11, 1986, 63 f.

[234] J. Fitzmyer, *op. cit.*, 950.

[235] See J. Jeremias, *Heiligengräber in Jesu Umwelt*, 1958, passim; O.H. Steck, *Israel und das gewaltsame Geschick der Propheten*, 1967, passim. - For the opinion that 1 Thess 2:13-16 is an interpolation, see B.A. Pearson, "1 Thessalonians 2,13-16: A Deutero-Pauline Interpolation", *HTR* 64, 1971, 79-94; D. Schmidt, "1 Thess 2:13–16: Linguistic Evidence for an Interpolation", *JBL* 102, 1983, 269–279.

Now those addressed by Jesus in Mt 23:32 are exhorted to fill up the measure of their fathers: πληρώσατε τὸ μέτρον τῶν πατέρων ὑμῶν. In other contexts it can be said that people fill up the measure of their sins (e.g. 1 Thess 2:16).[236] But that is not the case here. It is not the measure of wickedness in broad terms that is in focus. It is the 'measure of the forebears'. And in its context in Mt 23 that means that it is a question of the forefathers' rejection of the prophets and their killing of God's messengers to his people. That is the 'measure' the scribes and Pharisees are ironically exhorted to fill.[237]

In connection with this,[238] follows (after the ominous question in v. 33) an announcement of judgement introduced in the prophetic fashion by διὰ τοῦτο[239]. Jesus' representatives, bearers of the message about him and his works, will be struck and some even be killed, and therefore 'this γενεά' will be condemned (Mt 23:34-36). It is emphasized that they are Jesus' messengers. He is the one who sends. That is specifically stated and given extra stress by the emphatic ἐγώ (v. 34a).

In par. Lk 11:49 ἡ σοφία τοῦ θεοῦ is given as the sending subject: "Therefore also God's Wisdom said, 'I will send them prophets and apostles'..." No matter how ἡ σοφία τοῦ θεοῦ is to be understood here,[240] this passage is obviously also meant to refer to Jesus' messengers. As to the connection backwards, the wisdom-saying is coupled to the preceding 'woe', which means that the application of the saying to the situation described in the 'woe' is attributed to Jesus.[241] And for-

---

[236] Cf. Dan 8:23; 2 Macc 6:14; *Bib.Ant.* 26:13; 36:1; 41:1; *Gos.Pet.*17; *Barn.* 5:11; *Diogn.* 9:2.

[237] For the theme 'fill up the measure' see H. Ljungman, *Das Gesetz erfüllen*, 1954, passim; C.F.D. Moule, "Fulfilment–Words in the New Testament: Use and Abuse", *NTS* 14, 1968, 293–320. As for the implications of the exhortation to 'fill up the measure of the fathers' see further below.

[238] As for the belonging together of Mt 23:29–33 (par. Lk 11:47–48) and Mt 23:34–36 (par. Lk 11:49–51) cf. R.J. Miller, "The Rejection of the Prophets in Q", *JBL* 107, 1988, 227 f.

[239] The διὰ τοῦτο as an introduction to the judgement corresponds to לָכֵן (LXX: διὰ τοῦτο) in Is 5:24; Jer 23:2; Amos 3:11 *et al.* and is "a structural element in the prophetic announcement of judgment" (R.J. Miller, *op. cit.*, 227); cf. D. Lührmann, *Die Redaktion der Logienquelle*, 1969, 46; S. Schulz, *Q. Die Spruchquelle der Evangelisten*, 1972, 341 (with ref.); I.H. Marshall, *The Gospel of Luke*, 1978, 502; H. Schürmann, "Die Redekomposition wider 'dieses Geschlecht'", *SNTU* Ser. A, Bd 11, 1986, 55.

[240] There are divided opinions among scholars in this matter. A good review of the different opinions can be found in I.H. Marshall, *op. cit.*, 502-504. Cf. D.E. Garland, *The Intention of Matthew 23*, 1979, 172–174; J. Fitzmyer, *The Gospel according to Luke X-XXIV*, 1985, 943 f.; 950.

wards, the words about God's Wisdom sending 'prophets and apostles' and about the fate they will meet with, lead to the judgement required of 'this γενεά' (v. 50b[242]; par. Mt 23:35: it will come ἐφ' ὑμᾶς).[243] The emissaries are also spoken of in the terms used of leaders in the primitive Christian churches.[244]

The designations used for those sent differ partly in Mt and Lk respectively. In Mt they are talked of as 'prophets and wise men and scribes' (23:34)[245] and in Lk as 'prophets and apostles' (11:49). In both cases 'prophets' are thus mentioned first.[246] This should be seen against the background that the Old Testament prophets and their treatment are focused in the context (Mt 23:29–31; Lk 11:47–50). Here the explanation is apparently to be found as to why Lk has 'prophets and apostles'[247] in that order, while they appear in the reverse order otherwise in the New Testament (1 Cor 12:28; Eph 2:20; 3:5; 4:11; Rev 18:20). In Mt with its Jewish orientation, those sent by Jesus are referred to by a terminolgy with a stronger Jewish affinity.[248]

The point is that those sent out to bear the message of God's eschatalogical works of salvation through Jesus will meet resistance and be pursued and even killed. When, in both Gospels, it is first declared that some of them will be killed (ἀποκτείνειν), it should be seen in a similar way as above as a reference to the fates of the Old Testament prophets, referred to in the contexts. Moreover it is foretold in Mt that

---

[241] Cf. D.R.A. Hare, *The Theme of Jewish Persecution of Christians in the Gospel according to St. Matthew*, 1967, 86 f.

[242] O.H. Steck's opinion of ἀπὸ τῆς γενεᾶς ταύτης at that place as "eine nachlukanische, frühe Abschreiberglosse" is not convincing (*Israel und das gewaltsame Geschick der Propheten*, 1967, 32 n.1); see e.g. P. Hoffmann, *Studien zur Theologie der Logienquelle*, 1972, 167. Cf. D.R.A. Hare, *op.cit.*, 84: "The Wisdom-saying... seems not to have in mind any particular religious group (the Pharisees or their scribes) but rather the eschatological generation (τῆς γενεᾶς ταύτης, *bis* Luke 11:50 f.)".

[243] Cf. R.J. Miller, "The Rejection of the Prophets in Q", *JBL* 107, 1988, 230 f.

[244] Cf. C.F. Evans, *Saint Luke*, 1990, 508.

[245] Cf. D.E. Garland, *The Intention of Matthew 23*, 1979, 174–178.

[246] As for prophets and prophecy in early Christianity see e.g. David E. Aune, *Prophecy in Early Christianity and the Ancient Mediterranean World*, 1983.

[247] It is difficult to decide with certainty if ἀπόστολος here means 'apostle' or 'emissary'; cf. J. Fitzmyer, *op. cit.*, 950.

[248] Regarding the designations σοφός and γραμματεύς in ancient Judaism see G. Dalman, *Jesus–Jeschua*, 1922, 28; cf. B.T. Viviano, "Social World and Community Leadership: The Case of Matthew 23.1-12, 34", *JSNT* 39, 1990, 14 f.

some will be crucified[249] and some flogged in Jewish synagogues and persecuted from city to city (23:34), while Lk says in more general terms that some will be persecuted (11:49).[250]

It is this fate of the messengers that is in focus. In Mt 23:34 ff. the thoughts can be expressed as follows: Because you are of the same spiritual nature as your ancestors who killed the OT prophets - and in the perspective of your filling up the measure of your fathers - I send you prophets and wise men and scribes, and the result will be that they too (like the former prophets) will be persecuted and even killed, that (ὅπως) upon you may come... And in Lk 11:49 ff. (with its reference to the Wisdom) in this way: Because you, like your ancestors are at heart prophet-murderers, the Wisdom of God said,[251] I will send them prophets and apostles, and the result will be that some of those they will kill and others they will persecute, that (ἵνα[252]) of 'this *genea*' may be required...[253] For a further discussion of the meaning, see below.

In both Gospels the passages about those sent, lead up to an announcement of judgement, and in both cases it is 'this *genea*' which is struck. In Lk that is pointed out twice, both in vs. 50 and 51. In Mt 23:35 Jesus says to his addressees that the punishment will come 'upon you', but the spiritual leaders (scribes and Pharisees) he talks to are clearly seen as representatives for ἡ γενεὰ αὕτη, and in the summarising judgement in v. 36 that is what is stressed: "Truly, I say to you, all this will come upon 'this *genea*'". The judgement will strike 'this *genea*'. And this judgement will be radical. Both Gospels are in agreement here, although the formulation varies somewhat. In Lk the passage runs:

---

[249] Crucifixion was a Roman penalty. The Jews had not the right to carry out a death penalty passed by the Council (cf. Jn 18:31), without it being confirmed by the Roman governor. Then crucifixion was possible, which is demonstrated by the treatment of Jesus; cf. Mt 27:22 f. par Mk 15:13 f.; Lk 23:21 ff.; Jn 19:6,15; Acts 2:36; 4:10.

[250] Cf. Acts 7:52, where the verb 'persecute' is used with reference to the Old Testament prophets.

[251] It is not apparent how far the σοφία saying is meant to reach; cf. R.J. Miller, "The Rejection of the Prophets in Q", *JBL* 107, 1988, 229.

[252] Cf. W. Bauer, *Wörterbuch*, ⁶1988, sub ἵνα: "In vielen Fällen ist Absicht und Folge nicht streng geschieden und daher mit ἵνα d. Folge als der Absicht des Subj. od. Gottes entsprechend bez. Bes. bei göttl. Willensentscheidungen ist wie für Juden und Heiden ... Absicht und Erfolg identisch: Lk 11,50..." R.J. Miller refers as a parallel to Isaiah's situation according to Is 6:9-10 (where the prophet is sent to preach to the people in order that God will *not* heal them; cf. Mk 4:12 par.) and says: "This context blunts some of the bitter irony of the ἵνα, for it enables us to take it as signaling a less specific consecutive clause rather than a strict purpose clause" (*op. cit.*, 232).

[253] Cf. *Barn.* 5:11; 14:5.

"... that the blood of all the prophets which has been shed since the foundation of the world may be required of 'this γενεά', from the blood of Abel to the blood of Zechariah, who perished between the altar and the sanctuary. Yes, I tell you, it shall be required of 'this γενεά'" (11:50 f.).

Mt has this wording:

"...that upon you may come all the righteous blood shed on earth[254], from the blood of righteous Abel to the blood of Zechariah, *the son of Barachiah*, whom you murdered between the sanctuary and the altar. Truly I say to you, all this will come upon 'this γενεά'" (23:35 f.).

Instead of Lk's 'the blood of all the prophets' Mt uses the formulation 'all the righteous blood' shed on earth[255], a phrase through which Abel is not directly counted to the prophets[256] while he, however, is expressly described as 'righteous' (δίκαιος)[257].

When in Lk Zechariah is mentioned 'who perished between the altar and the sanctuary', he is generally and rightly taken to be Zechariah, the son of Jehoiada, who was, according to 2 Chron 24:17-22, stoned "in the court of the house of the Lord". In this OT passage we are told that God had repeatedly sent prophets to the king (Joash) and the people to bring them back to the Lord, but in vain. Then the Spirit of God took possession of (*lit.* 'clothed itself with') Zechariah, who as God's mouth-piece addressed the people. But on orders from the king they stoned him to death. Zechariah was a priest[258], but considering that God's spirit worked through him, he was looked on in Jewish tradition as a prophet as well. Josephus thus says that God had appointed him to prophesy (προφητεύειν; *Ant.* IX,8:3 § 168 f.), and in *Targ. 2 Chron.* 24:20 the

---

[254] Cf. the expression in Mt 27:25: "His blood be on us"...

[255] Some scholars interpret ἡ γῆ as referring to the 'land' of Israel (e.g. A.H. M'Neile, *The Gospel according to St. Matthew*, 1915 [1965], 339; J. Gnilka, *Das Matthäusevangelium* II, 1988, 300 f.), but the reference to Abel which follows immediately after hardly supports this interpretation.

[256] Abel was of course not a prophet in the current sense of the word, but cf. J. Fitzmyer, *op. cit.*, 951: "Though Abel was not a prophet, the use of this saying by Luke fits his general view of the OT in which most of it is regarded as some sort of prophecy".

[257] Regarding the righteousness of Abel see e.g. Heb 11:4: "By faith Abel offered to God a more acceptable sacrifice than Cain, through which he received approval as righteous (δίκαιος), God bearing witness by accepting his gifts". Cf. *1 Enoch* 22:7–9. Josephus also emphasizes Abel's righteousness (*Ant.* I,2:1 § 53). Cf. *T. Iss.* 5:4, where Abel is mentioned as the first one among the saints (οἱ ἅγιοι).

[258] Since Jehoiada was a priest (2 Chron 24:20a), his son can also be assumed to have been one. This is taken for granted in ancient Jewish literature; cf. M. McNamara, *The New Testament and the Palestinian Targum to the Pentateuch*, 1966, 162, and see ref. below.

Spirit's taking possession of him is rendered in the following manner: "The Spirit *of prophecy* from IHWH (רוּחַ נְבוּאָה מִן קֳדָם יְיָ) dwelt on Zechariah".[259] He is also included in *Vitae Prophetarum* (first century A.D.[260]).

In Mt, Zechariah is now referred to as 'the son of Barachiah' (υἱὸς Βαραχίου). Otherwise in principle the same things are said about him here as in Luke:..."whom you murdered between the sanctuary and the altar" (23:35). But Mt's patronymic creates problems. How is it to be interpreted? That is an important question in this connection.

Is it possible that it is the eleventh of the Minor Prophets that is meant? In Zech 1:1,7 his full title is 'Zechariah the son of Berechiah, son of Iddo' (LXX: Ζαχαρίας ὃς τοῦ Βαραχίου υἱὸς Ἀδδώ). How-ever, nothing is known about him that suggests that he died a violent death, and even less that it should have happened 'between the sanctuary and the altar'.[261] There is thus no relevant information in his case that corresponds to the important identification of the Zechariah given in Mt 23:35.

Some scholars hold that Matthew is referring to Ζαχαρίας υἱὸν Βάρεις, who is mentioned by Josephus in *Bell.* IV, 5:4, § 334-344.[262] Josephus tells us that Zacharias - 'one of the most eminent of the citizens' - was accused of treasonable communications with the Romans. The accusers were Zealots. They called in seventy leading citizens to the Temple where they were - as in a play - to function as judges. The seventy, however, acquitted him. Then two of the Zealots "set upon Zacharias and slew him in the midst of the Temple (ἐν μέσῳ τῷ ἱερῷ) and... cast him out of the Temple into the ravine below". This happened c. year 68.

Can this be the Zacharias that is referred to in Mt 23:35? There are several problems in connection with that interpretation. If the patro-nymic there does not agree with that of Zechariah in 2 Chron 24:20-22, nor does it agree with the name used by Josephus: instead of Mt's υἱὸς

---

[259] As examples of passages where Zechariah the son of Jehoiada is talked about as a prophet can be mentioned *b. Git.* 57b; *b. Sanh.* 96b. See further Str-B 1, 940-942 (ref.).

[260] See e.g. D.R.A. Hare in *OTP* II, 1985, 380 f.

[261] Cf. S.H. Blank, "The Death of Zechariah in Rabbinic Literature", *HUCA* XII-XIII, 1937-1938, 334; *Tg. Lam.* 2:20 refers without doubt to Zechariah the son of Jehoiada; see M. McNamara, *op. cit.*, 162 f.

[262] E.g. O.H. Steck, *Israel und das gewaltsame Geschick der Propheten*, 1967, 39 f.; R. Walker, *Die Heilsgeschichte im ersten Evangelium*, 1967, 57 f.; J. Gnilka, *Das Matthäusevangelium* II, 1988, 301 f.

Βαραχίου the Josephus text has υἱὸς Βάρεις (v.l. Βαρούχου, Βαρισκαί-ου). Furthermore it is said that the Zechariah referred to in Mt should have been murdered 'between the sanctuary and the altar', that is in the court of the priests. It is improbable that that could apply to Zacharias in Josephus Bell. Josephus does not identify him as a priest, so that he could have had admittance to this court. Nor are the seventy 'judges' called in, identified as priests. Zacharias was killed at the tribunal set up in the Temple.[263] Furthermore it is not probable that Matthew would have put into Jesus' mouth words about something that people knew had happened decades later - his saying about the deed against Zechariah the son of Barachiah is not a prophecy but talks about something that has happened[264], and the murder of Zacharias by the Zealots shortly before the fall of Jerusalem must have been known to many. The opinion that Mt meant the Zacharias, son of Baris, spoken of by Josephus, is therefore not convincing.[265]

What then is the case regarding Zechariah the son of Jehoiada (2 Chron 24:20-22)? Can it be he who is meant after all? It appears that, in the ancient traditions, there exists some variation and confusion regarding the patronymics of the different Zechariahs. The prophet Zechariah in Zech 1:1 is not normally called 'Zechariah the son of Berechiah'; in all three passages (outside Zech 1:1) where he is mentioned in the Old Testament, he is talked of as 'Zechariah the son of Iddo' (Ezra 5:1; 6:14; Neh 12:16).[266] In Is 8:2, the Zechariah mentioned there has the patronymic Jeberechiah (יְבֶרֶכְיָהוּ), which is in the LXX rendered by Barachiah (Βαραχίας), the same as in LXX Zech 1:1[267] and Mt 23:35. Of special interest here is Targ. Lam. 2:20, where it reads:

"Is it proper to kill in the Temple of the Lord a priest and a prophet as you killed Zechariah bar Iddo the high priest and the faithful prophet in the Temple of the Lord on the day of atonement, because he admonished you not to do what was evil before the Lord?"

It is quite clear from the description that it is Zechariah, the son of Jehoiada who is intended here.[268] But the designation of the Zechariah

---

[263] Cf. M. McNamara, op.cit., 161.

[264] ...ὃν ἐφονεύσατε, ... "whom you murdered" (Mt 23:35).

[265] Cf. D.E. Garland, The Intention of Matthew 23, 1979, 182 f.

[266] Cf. M. McNamara, The New Testament and the Palestinian Targum to the Pentateuch, 1966, 162. In the same way in e.g. b. 'Erub. 21a; b. Yoma 39b.

[267] In b. Mak. 24b Zechariah, son of Jeberechiah (Is 8:2) is identified with the prophet Zechariah (Zech 1:1) in a saying that is traced back to R. Akiba (d. c. 135). Cf. S.H. Blank, op. cit., 328–330.

[268] Cf. M. McNamara, op. cit., 162 f.

who gave his name to the prophetic book, 'Zechariah, the son of Iddo' (see above) is used about him. Taking this background into consideration, it would not in any way be unique if there was also confusion in Mt 23:35 as to the patronymic of the Zechariah referred to, so that it is Zechariah, the son of Jehoiada who is meant there.

The information that it is about the Zechariah who was murdered between the sanctuary and the altar, thus in the court of the priests, then becomes essential. This definitely points at Zechariah, the son of Jehoiada. The fate that he suffered has apparently occupied the thoughts of the people of ancient Judaism. The numerous passages in the rabbinic literature which deal with it bear witness to that.[269] Regarding the place for his murder it is said in 2 Chron 24:21 that he was stoned "in the court of the house of the Lord". It is reasonable to assume that *the court of the house* of the Lord' refers to the court of the priests, where the altar for the burnt offerings was situated, in front of the temple building. This is also the interpretation we find in rabbinical writings. In a saying (with several par.) for instance, the direct question is asked: "Where did they kill Zechariah? In the court of the women or in the court of the ordinary Israelites?" And R. Acha (c. 320) gives the answer: "In neither of these but in the court of the priests".[270]

The confusion of the patronymics of the Old Testament Zechariahs found in Jewish literature on the one hand and the identification of Zechariah, the son of Barachiah in Mt 23:35 as having been murdered between the sanctuary and the altar on the other hand support in a decisive fashion the view that it is Zechariah, the son of Jehoiada that is really meant in Matthew as well as in Luke.[271] The specification thus means in both Gospels: from the blood of Abel to the blood of Zechariah, who according to 2 Chron 24:21 was stoned in the court of the house of the Lord.

Considering the context in the Gospels it is worth noting that the Scripture in both these cases speaks of vengeance. The blood of Abel cried to God from the ground (Gen 4:10), and when Zechariah was

---

[269] See e.g. Str-B 1, 940 ff.; S.H. Blank, *op. cit.*, 335 ff.; J. Jeremias, *op. cit.*, 67.

[270] *p. Ta'an.* IV, 9 (69a); par. *Lam. Rab.* Introd. V (2b); *Eccles. Rab.* III, 16:1 (11b–12a); X, 3:1 (26a).

[271] This is the opinion of a large number of scholars, e.g. A.H. M'Neile, *The Gospel according to St. Matthew*, 1915 (repr. 1965), 340; Str-B 1, 940 ff.; F.V. Filson, *A Commentary on the Gospel according to St. Matthew*, 1960, 248; M. McNamara, *op. cit.*, 162 f.; E. Schweizer, *Das Evangelium nach Matthäus*, 1973, 290; D.E. Garland, *The Intention of Matthew 23*, 1979, 182 f. – Cf. Hieronymus, *Comm. in Matth.* 23,35 *ff.* (regarding the Gospel of the Hebrews): "In Evangelio quo utuntur Nazareni, pro 'filio Barachiae', 'filium Joiadae' reperimus scriptum".

dying he said: "May the Lord see and avenge!" (2 Chron 24:22).[272]

2 Chronicles is the final book in the Hebrew Bible. It is true that we have no guarantee that the order of the books was the same in primitive Christianity as it is today. But there is old information that at an early stage 2 Chron was placed last among the books of the Scripture[273], and one might argue from the reference in question with its ἀπό... ἕως... that it did.[274] Jesus' specification 'from Abel to Zechariah' meant then: from the first to the last prophet[275] spoken of in the first and last books of the Hebrew Bible as murdered. Among those who understand the Zechariah of the passage in question as here, this is the usual interpretation, and it is no doubt also the correct one.[276]

This then means that the reference is to a period long since over. There is a substantial time between the death of the last prophetic martyr in the OT and the era of 'this *genea*'.[277] How can that be?[278] If it was a matter of a general accumulation of guilt as is often assumed, the sense would seem to require that the speaker covered the whole period up to the time of speaking, the time of 'this *genea*'.[279] It would have been natural to mention John the Baptist or Jesus or the messengers who according to the *logion* were going to be killed, instead of mentioning Zechariah. But this is not the case.

If Zechariah in the Mt text referred to the Zacharias who was killed

---

[272] For the Jewish legend of the blood of the murdered Zechariah see S.H. Blank, *op. cit.*, 336 ff.

[273] In a Baraitha in *b. B.B.* 14b it is said: "The order of the Hagiographa is Ruth, the Book of Psalms, Job, Prophets, Ecclesiastes, Song of Songs, Lamentations, Daniel and the Scroll of Ester, Ezra and Chronicles".

[274] Cf. O.H. Steck, *Israel und das gewaltsame Geschick der Propheten*, 1967, 37. – 'From the blood of Abel to the blood of Zechariah' cannot refer *chronologically* to the first and last murder of a prophet that the Hebrew Bible knows of, as e.g. the murder of the prophet Uriah, the son of Shemaiah was later than that of Zechariah (Jer 26:20-23).

[275] As for Abel, see above.

[276] E.g. A.H. M'Neile, *op. cit.*, 340; K.H. Rengstorf, *Das Evangelium nach Lukas*, 1962, 155; W. Grundmann, *Das Evangelium nach Matthäus*, 1968, 495; D. Lührmann, *Die Redaktion der Logienquelle*, 1969, 47; E. Schweizer, *op. cit.*, 290; S. Légasse, *op. cit.*, 250; J. Fitzmyer, *The Gospel according to Luke X–XXIV*, 1985, 946.

[277] Regarding 'this *genea*' as supposed to refer to the Jewish people, see below.

[278] Cf. E.E. Ellis: "It is strange that Jesus (or the 'Q' tradition) should limit the guilt to 'canonical' murders" (*The Gospel of Luke*, 1981, 173 f.).

[279] Cf. C.F. Evans, *Saint Luke*, 1990, 509. – Cf. *T. Iss.* 5:4, where it is said that the Lord has blessed all the saints ἀπὸ Ἀβὲλ ἕως τοῦ νῦν.

in the Temple c. 68, according to Josephus, the situation in this respect would be different. Then the specification 'from Abel to Zechariah' would encompass the time up until shortly before the Fall of Jerusalem. This interpretation has, however, not been found acceptable (see above).

Another suggested solution to this problem is that 'this *genea*' applies to Israel's unrepentent people.[280] The specification 'from the blood of Abel to the blood of Zechariah' has then some times been seen as an accentuation that it is a matter of innocent blood spilled in *Israel*.[281] According to this interpretation it is said in the passage that the Jewish people will be struck by God's punishment for their rejection and persecution of God's messengers, which they have carried out in the past and still carry out at present. However, this interpretation does not get any support from what has been established above concerning the use and content of the term 'this *genea*' in synoptic texts.

It has been shown that the phrase is there seen from a salvation-historical perspective. The formulation applies to the γενεά which has as its characteristic that people have experienced the fulfilment of the OT prophesies and the arrival of the predicted Saviour, Jesus, but have adopted a negative, rejecting attitude to him. That is important for our understanding of the texts in question.

As pointed out above (p. 68 f.) in the 'woe', to which the *logion* in Mt 23:34-36 par. Lk 11:49-51 connects, there is no mention that the forefathers were unrighteous in general terms but that they killed the prophets (Mt 23:29-33 par. Lk 11:47 f.) - as well as 'the prophets' Mt names 'the righteous' (v. 29). And in the judgement in question it is said in Lk that 'the blood of all the prophets' may be required of 'this *genea*' (11:50 f.), while Mt, as noted, uses the formulation 'all the righteous blood' shed on earth with the subsequent determination ἀπὸ τοῦ αἵματος ᾿Αβελ ἕως τοῦ αἵματος Ζαχαρίου (23:35). It is the forefathers' attacks on and killing of the prophets and the righteous[282] that are emphasized. And the specification 'from Abel to Zechariah' brings the scriptural reference into focus.

According to the early Christian view the OT Scriptures look forward, manifestly or implicitly, and Jesus is seen as the Messianic

---

[280] E.g. F. Prat, "Cette génération", *RSR* 17, 1927, 320; J. Schniewind, *Das Evangelium nach Matthäus*, 1954, 237; Max Meinertz, "'Dieses Geschlecht' im Neuen Testament", *BZ* N.F. 1, 1957, 286 f.; K.H. Rengstorf, *op. cit.*, 151, 155 f.; P. Bonnard, *L'Évangile selon Saint Matthieu*, 1963, 342; D. Lührmann, *Die Redaktion der Logienquelle*, 1969, 30, 46-48.

[281] D. Lührmann, *op. cit.*, 47. For a criticism of Lührmann's interpretation see P. Hoffmann, *Studien zur Theologie der Logienquelle*, 1972, 168 f.

[282] As for 'the righteous' – 'the Righteous One' see below.

fulfilment of Scripture.[283] The prophets' predictions about the coming eschatological Saviour have been fulfilled in him, and if it talks of righteous men in the Old Testament, he is the Righteous One (par excellence). A passage at the end of Stephen's speech to the Sanhedrin is illuminating in this context. Stephen addresses the members of the court with the accusation that they always resist the Holy Spirit; as their fathers did, so do they. And he continues: "Which of the prophets did not your fathers persecute? And they killed those who announced beforehand the coming of the Righteous One, whom you have now betrayed and murdered" (Acts 7:51 f.). Here reference is made, as in the passages in question in the Gospels, to the forefathers' persecution of the prophets, and in connection with that it is emphasized that they killed those who foretold the coming of the Saviour. And he is referred to as ὁ δίκαιος, 'the Righteous One'. Finally it is stated that he has now been betrayed and murdered by them. Just as in the Gospel texts, this is an example of the same negative attitude to God's messengers from the contemporary representatives of Israel as their forefathers once held. Here it is summarised as resistance to the Holy Spirit. Regarding the relationship between the deeds of the forefathers and those of the people who represent Israel in the situation in Stephen's speech, it is described in the perspective of an announcement beforehand/fulfilment: The fathers persecuted the prophets and killed those who foretold the coming of the Righteous One, and he has now been murdered by Stephen's adversaries.

It is, of course, a fact that the realities of fulfilment in Jesus' mission and deeds in the New Testament are greater than the models in the Old Testament. "What is here is greater than Jonah" (Mt 12:41 par.). "What is here is greater than Solomon" (Mt 12:42 par.). We are told of righteous men in the Scripture, but Jesus is *the* Righteous One (Acts 7:52). As C.F.D. Moule puts it: "Thus, to a unique degree, Jesus is seen as the goal, the convergence-point, of God's plan for Israel, his covenant-promise".[284] With him all that the Law and the Prophets stood for is brought to its final conclusion.[285] This means that those to whom it is given to experience God's works of salvation through Jesus also

---

[283] Cf. E. Lövestam, "Urkyrkans skriftförståelse" in *Axplock*, 1987, 17–25, with references.

[284] "Fulfilment-Words in the New Testament: Use and Abuse", *NTS* 14, 1968, 301.

[285] Cf. C.F.D. Moule, *op. cit.*, 314. Cf. the Jewish expectations regarding the eschatological prophet, put thus by O. Cullmann: The hope of the return of prophecy at the end of time "hatte bereits auch die konkrete Form der Überzeugung angenommen, es werde *ein* Prophet am Ende erscheinen, der sozusagen die Erfüllung aller früheren Prophetie darstellt" (*Die Christologie des Neuen Testaments*, 2. Aufl., 1958, 14).

have a much greater responsibility. It is expressed in the texts mentioned above as well as in many other passages, e.g. that of Jesus' upbraiding of the Galilean towns in which most of his mighty works had been done (Mt 11:20-24).

This is no doubt how the gospel texts in question are to be understood. When Jesus in Mt 23:32 ironically exhorts the scribes and Pharisees to fill up the measures of their fathers, who murdered the prophets, it is not just a matter of a continuing accumulation of unrighteousness and guilt throughout the history of the people up until 'this (the last) generation'. In accordance with the meaning of ἡ γενεὰ αὕτη in the Synoptics it is about filling up the measure of their fathers in the sense that they persecute and kill the messengers of him who is the fulfilment of the prophetically given promises in the Scriptures about the eschatological Saviour.

The saying that all the righteous blood shed on earth, from Abel to Zechariah, will come upon 'this *genea*', should be seen and understood from this point of view. It is important that the specification 'from Abel to Zechariah' here manifestly refers to the Scriptures. What is told there about prophets and righteous men is part of God's dealings with his people. But, as was emphasized above, that is not God's final salvation event, it carries the future with it, it points ahead. And now, according to the early Christian view the prophesied eschatological IHWH event has arrived with Jesus and his words and deeds - the difference in relation to the realities of the Old Testament in this respect is often described in terms of wholeness and completeness.[286] The filling up of 'the fathers' measure' in the Mt passage, i.e. the rejection of the representatives of the act of God that is given with Jesus, he who is the fulfilment of the Scriptures[287], is seen then as also including the rejection of the Scripture's prophets and righteous men who have predicted him and pointed forwards to him. The starting point in the Mt passage is that the addressees - representatives of 'this *genea*' - wish, with words and actions, to disavow the malicious deeds of their fathers against the prophets (Mt 23:29 f.). Now they are told that they are of the same spiritual character and cannot avoid judgement (v. 33). On the contrary, 'all righteous blood' – ἀπὸ ᾽Αβελ ἕως Ζαχαρίου — which according to the Scriptures, has been shed on earth will come upon ἡ γενεὰ αὕτη. For the dismissive and agressive attitude to God's chosen

---

[286] Cf. C.F.D. Moule, *op. cit.*, 295.

[287] Cf. Acts 3:24, where, after applying the words of Moses about the coming prophet to Jesus, Peter says, "And all the prophets from Samuel on, as many as have spoken, have foretold these days".

ones that the Scriptures bear witness to, from Gen to 2 Chron, reaches its full measure with the rejection of and attacks on Jesus and his messengers by 'this *genea*'.

In Lk it is likewise stated that Jesus' addressees distinguish themselves by having the same attitude to God's envoys as their fathers. They consent to the deeds of their fathers, those who killed the prophets (Lk 11:47 f.). In connection with that comes the judgement introduced by διὰ τοῦτο (see above) and a reference to what God's Wisdom has said about sending them prophets and apostles, some of whom they will persecute and kill. They will behave in the same way towards them as their fathers did towards the prophets. Their attitude of rejection and agressivity will be manifested, and that against the messengers of God's Wisdom/Jesus at the time of fulfilment. In Lk it is also, in this way, a case of filling up the forbears' measure, even if that formulation is not used. Considering the meaning of the ἡ γενεὰ αὕτη terminology in the Gospels shown here, this aspect is also expressed in a way through the use of the phrase 'this *genea*', which in contrast to the parallel passage in Mt is introduced as early as in v. 50. The consequences are disastrous. The judgement that the blood of all the prophets, shed from the foundation of the world, may be required of 'this *genea*', is to be understood in the same way as the par. passage in Mt.

It should be noted that the phrase ἡ γενεὰ αὕτη here also includes those who reject Jesus' emissaries, just as in Mt 11:16 ff. par. Lk 7:31 ff. it includes those who distance themselves from the forerunner. This further emphasizes its salvation-historical orientation. The term is related to the eschatological act of salvation in Jesus, beginning with the precursor and after Jesus going further with the messengers sent out by him.

Finally it should be emphasized that in the light of the *dor/genea* idea in question in early Judaism and in the synoptic Gospels, the radical judgement on ἡ γενεὰ αὕτη in Mt 23:35 f. par. Lk 11: 50 f. should not be interpreted as if the door to repentance had now been closed so that all that remained was the punishment. In this respect, what has been stated earlier regarding the judgement on 'this *genea*' in Mt 12:41 f. par. Lk 11:31 f. is valid even here; see above p. 37.

8. " Ἡ γενεὰ αὕτη will not pass away until all these Things take Place"

The statement quoted in the heading is part of Jesus' eschatological discourse in Mk 13 (par. Mt 24; Lk 21). This section has been the object of several investigations in later times.[288] Following the parable of the fig tree, the saying shows only small variations in the three synoptic Gospels.[289] Mt and Lk have ἕως ἄν πάντα ταῦτα (Lk: πάντα) γένη-ται for Mk's μέχρις οὗ ταῦτα πάντα γένηται. Otherwise the wording is identical.[290] The discussion of the logion has mainly concentrated on the phrases ταῦτα πάντα and ἡ γενεὰ αὕτη and their significations.[291]

Firstly, what is meant by ταῦτα πάντα? The discourse in Mk 13 par. has a complicated structure, with different interwoven components. Taking this into consideration, some scholars believe it possible that the phrase refers to the events up to the destruction of Jerusalem.[292] Others associate it with the signs of the End described in vs. 5–23: they are characteristic of the whole period of the last times, and therefore Jesus' hearers must themselves experience them.[293] It seems, however, inevi-

---

[288] E.g. L. Hartman, *Prophecy Interpreted. The Formation of some Jewish Apocalyptic Texts and of the Eschatological Discourse Mark 13 par.* (ConBNT 1), 1966; J. Lambrecht, *Die Redaktion der Markus-Apokalypse* (AnBib 28), 1967; R. Pesch, *Naherwartungen. Tradition und Redaktion in Mk 13*, 1968; F. Hahn, "Die Rede von der Parusie des Menschensohnes Markus 13", *Jesus und der Menschensohn* (FS A. Vögtle), 1975, 240–266; E. Brandenburger, *Markus 13 und die Apokalyptik* (FRLANT 134), 1984; D. Wenham, *The Rediscovery of Jesus' Eschatological Discourse,* 1984; J. Dupont, *Les trois apocalypses synoptiques. Marc 13; Matthieu 24–25; Luc 21* (LD 121), 1985; G. Beasley-Murray, *Jesus and the Last Days*, 1993 (with a comprehensive review of research).

[289] Regarding this saying cf. E. Lövestam, "The ἡ γενεὰ αὕτη Eschatology in Mk 13,30 parr.", *L'Apocalypse johannique et l'Apocalyptique dans le Nouveau Testament* (BETL 53), 1980, 403–413.

[290] There are indications that the saying was originally formulated in a Semitic language; cf. K. Beyer, *Semitische Syntax im Neuen Testament* (SUNT 1), Bd I:1, 132 f.

[291] As for the history of the interpretation of Mark 13:30 par. see M. Künzi, *Das Naherwartungslogion Markus 9,1 par*, 1977, 213–224.

[292] E.g. M.-J. Lagrange, *Evangile selon Saint Marc* (Ebib), 1947, 348; A. Feuillet, "Le discours de Jésus sur la ruine du temple d'après Marc XIII et Luc XXI, 5-36", *RB* 55, 1948, 481-502 and 56, 1949, 61-92 (see p. 84); B. Nolan, "Some Observations on the Parousia and New Testament Eschatology", *ITQ* 36, 1969, 296–300; D. Wenham, *op. cit.*, 333. Cf G.R. Beasley-Murray, *Jesus and the Last Days*, 1993, 445-449 (with ref.).

table that ταῦτα πάντα in its present context embraces the totality of eschatological events, including the *parousia* (Mk 13:26 f. par.). In Mk 13:30 par. it is then stated that ἡ γενεὰ αὕτη will not pass away before the end of the world and the *parousia* take place.[294]

Then ἡ γενεὰ αὕτη will be an evident problem. The term has been characterized as "in the long run the most difficult phrase to interpret in this complicated eschatological discourse".[295] To what does it refer? To Jesus' contemporaries, his 'generation' with the stress on the temporal aspect? This is a common interpretation.[296] However, it gives rise to some critical questions. How does it agree with the use of the expression elsewhere in the Synoptics? As has been seen above it is not the usual signification of the phrase in the gospel texts.[297] And how should one interpret the connection of Jesus' saying in Mk 13:30 par. with his subsequent radical statement about him having no knowledge of 'that day or that hour' (Mk 13:32 par. Mt 24:36)? This statement is of such a general character that it should be understood in an absolute sense: the time is unknown not only within a particular scope ('this generation') but totally and entirely.[298] It then constitutes a considerable problem regarding the interpretation of 'this *genea*' in question.[299]

---

[293] C.E.B. Cranfield, *The Gospel according to Saint Mark*, 1959, 409; cf. W. Michaelis, *Der Herr verzieht nicht die Verheissung*, 1942, 30 f.

[294] Cf. W.G. Kümmel, *Promise and Fulfilment*, 1957, 60; A. Vögtle, *Das Evangelium und die Evangelien*, 1971, 298; F. Hahn, *op. cit.*, 247; M. Künzi, *op. cit.*, 224; J. Dupont, *op. cit.*, 39, 69, 136; F. Mussner, "Wer ist 'dieses Geschlecht' in Mk 13,30 parr.?", *Kairos* NF 29, 1987, 24; J. Gnilka, *Das Matthäusevangelium* II, 1988, 336; I.H. Marshall, *The Gospel of Luke*, 1978, 780; E. Schweizer, *Das Evangelium nach Markus*, 1967, 161; J. Fitzmyer, *The Gospel according to Luke X–XXIV*, 1985, 1353; C.F. Evans, *Saint Luke*, 1990, 758. This is the opinion of most exegetes.

[295] J. Fitzmyer, *op. cit.*, 1353.

[296] Cf. A.H. M'Neile, *The Gospel according to St. Matthew*, 1915 (1965), 354 f.; E. Haenchen, *Der Weg Jesu*, 1966, 451; F. Hahn, *op. cit.*, 243. 245; M. Künzi, *op. cit.*, 224; R. Pesch, *Das Markusevangelium* II, 1977, 309; R. Maddox, *The Purpose of Luke–Acts*, 1982, 115; J. Gnilka, *Das Matthäusevangelium* II, 1988, 336. This interpretation is held by the majority of the exegetes.

[297] It does happen that the phrase is ascribed a different meaning in Mk 13:30 par. from elsewhere in the Synoptics; thus e.g. D. Lührmann: "αὕτη ἡ γενεά ... meint offenbar mit Ausnahme von Mk 13,30 parr das Volk Israel" (*Die Redaktion der Logienquelle*, 1969, 30). See below p. 85.

[298] E.g. M. Meinertz, "'Dieses Geschlecht' im Neuen Testament" , *BZ* NF 1, 1957, 287 f.; R. Schnackenburg, *Gottes Herrschaft und Reich*, 1961, 146; L. Oberlinner, "Die Stellung der 'Terminworte' in der eschatologischen Verkündigung des Neuen Testaments", in *Gegenwart und kommendes Reich* (FS A. Vögtle), 1975, 52.

[299] Some scholars suggest that 'this *genea*' is 'the generation of the end-signs'; cf. J. Fitzmyer, *The Gospel according to Luke X–XXIV*, 1985, 1353 (with ref. to H.

Other solutions have therefore also been suggested.

Can the phrase refer to the Jews as a race, a people? This is an old suggestion which has several advocates in later times.[300] The saying can then be regarded as a word of hope to the Jews in spite of their sin, as God does not want to abandon his people.[301] For this interpretation reference has been made to the use of the term in Mt 12:41 f. (par. Lk 11:31 f.) and in Mt 23:34-36 (par. Lk 11:49–51)[302]. But that is not convincing – for the use of the phrase in these passages see above chap. 3 and 7.[303] As far as the eschatological discourse is concerned, it is true that attention is directed to the temple of Jerusalem (Mk 13:1–3) and that it speaks about attacks in the synagogues (13:9) and about the flight to the mountains by those who are in Judea (13:14)[304], but the idea of Israel and its special relation to other peoples is not brought up in the context and it is thus difficult to find evidence in the speech itself to motivate the supposition that the statement in question should apply especially to the Jews.[305]

Can 'this *genea*' then mean the human race, mankind in general? This is also an old suggestion[306], and at least as far as the Gospel of Luke is concerned it can be found in a number of present-day exegetes.[307] Against this interpretation it has been rightly argued that the

Conzelmann and G. Schneider). E.E. Ellis is of this opinion and identifies 'the generation of the end-signs' with the 'generation of the end time', whose temporal extent he finds to be left indeterminate with ref. to 1QpHab 2:7 and 7:2 (see below); *The Gospel of Luke*, 1974 (1983), 246 f. It has also been claimed that the statement "this *genea* will not pass away before..." is to be seen from the point of view of the evangelist, not the speaker (e.g. E. Brandenburger, *Markus 13 und die Apokalyptik*, 1984, 120: "Die Lebenszeit einer Generation hat man mit etwa 30 Jahren anzusetzen. Das ist nicht vom Standort des Sprechers, sondern von dem des Markus aus zu betrachten"). For criticism of this see F. Mussner, "Wer ist 'dieses Geschlecht' in Mk 13,30 parr.?", *Kairos* 29, 1987, 24–25; cf. R. Maddox, *op. cit.*, 113 f.

[300] It goes back as far as Jerome (*In evang. Matth.* ad loc., MPL 26, 180); more recently see e.g. M. Meinertz, *op. cit.*, 287 f.; J. Schniewind, *Das Evangelium nach Markus*, 1958, 141 f.; K.H. Rengstorf, *Das Evangelium nach Lukas*, 1962, 238; F. Mussner, *op. cit.*, 23–28.

[301] Cf. K.H. Rengstorf, *op. cit.*, 238.

[302] Cf. M. Meinertz, *op. cit.*, 286 f.

[303] Cf. also R. Maddox, *The Purpose of Luke–Acts*, 1982, 111 f.

[304] Cf. F. Mussner, *op. cit.*, 26.

[305] Cf. W. Michaelis, *op. cit.*, 32; R. Schnackenburg, *Gottes Herrschaft und Reich*, 1961, 144 f. – Contra the interpretation of γενεά as 'race' with application to the Jewish people, J. Jeremias claims: "Die Bedeutung 'Rasse' kan griech. γενεά haben, nicht jedoch hebr. *dor* bzw. aram. *dar*" (*Neutestamentliche Theologie* I, 1971, 136).

[306] It is given as an alternative by Jerome (*ibid.*).

[307] See e.g. H. Conzelmann, *Die Mitte der Zeit*, 5. Aufl. 1964, 122 ("'Dieses Ge-

statement would be rather trite if it implied that mankind in general will not pass away until the end comes.[308]

It has also been suggested that ἡ γενεὰ αὕτη refers to the faithful, the Christians.[309] Or to 'this kind' in a more general sense, i.e. to mankind's evil nature, meaning that there will be unbelievers till the end.[310] However, it is difficult to find convincing reasons for any of those interpretations.[311]

As has been seen earlier the Dead Sea Scrolls talk about הַדּוֹר הָאַחֲרוֹן 'the final *dor*' (*genea*). Thus in 1QpHab 2:7 and 7:2. In 7:1 f. Habakkuk is said to have been told by God to write down that which is to come upon the final *dor*, but it is clearly stated that God did not make known to the prophet when time would come to an end (גְּמֵר הַקֵּץ). It is thus left open. And shortly afterwards it is said as a comment on Hab 2:3a that the final age (הַקֵּץ הָאַחֲרוֹן) shall be prolonged and shall exceed all that the prophets have said (7:7 f.).[312] הַדּוֹר הָאַחֲרוֹן here apparently corresponds to הַקֵּץ הָאַחֲרוֹן and is then characterized by the same openness regarding its extent. 'The final *dor*' is the *dor* of 'the final age' with its indeterminate temporal extent.[313]

The passages referred to in the Dead Sea writings demonstrate the

schlecht' ist hier vielleicht die Menschheit überhaupt, während man bei Mc zweifeln kann, wer gemeint sei"); A.R.C. Leaney, *A Commentary on the Gospel according to St. Luke*, 1966, 263; J. Zmijewski, *Die Eschatologiereden des Lukas-Evangeliums*, 1972, 281 f.

308 Cf. E. Schweizer, *Das Evangelium nach Markus*, 1967, 161 f.: "Verstände man hier ... in diesem Sinn, wäre der Satz eine Banalität; denn nirgends ist in einem zeitgenössischen Dokument inner- oder ausserhalb der Bibel mit der Möglichkeit gerechnet, dass die Menscheit vor dem Weltende aussterben könnte" Cf. C.F. Evans, *Saint Luke*, 1990, 759.

309 Chrysostom, *Comm. in Matth.* ad loc., MPG 57, 702; Eusebius, *Comm. in Luc* ad loc, MPG 24, 601 ff.; cf. O. Merk, who finds it most probable that the phrase in Lk 21:32 refers to "die Jüngerschar ..., die alle Katastrophen bis zum Ende durchhalten wird" ("Das Reich Gottes in den lukanischen Schriften", *Jesus und Paulus* [FS W.G. Kümmel], 1978, 218).

310 W. Michaelis, *Der Herr verzieht nicht die Verheissung*, 1942, 32 f.; cf. R. Gundry, *Matthew*, 1982, 491.

311 If ἡ γενεὰ αὕτη were to refer to the believers in Christ the phrase would here fall entirely outside the range of its prevalent use in the Synoptics, and that is hard to believe. As for Michaelis' suggestion that it should mean 'this (evil) kind' it seems that he himself had become doubtful about it; see G.R. Beasley-Murray, *A Commentary on Mark thirteen*, 1957, 100.

312 See K.G. Kuhn, "Die in Palästina gefundenen hebräisachen Texte und das Neue Testament", *ZTK* 47, 1950, 208 f.

313 Cf. J. Daniélou, "Eschatologie sadocite et eschatologie chrétienne", *Les manuscrits de la Mer Morte*, 1957, 121, where the importance of this for the understanding of the statement about 'this *genea*' in Mt 24:34 is claimed.

use of דור in an end-time perspective in early Jewish scriptures and, at the same time, show the elasticity of the temporal extent of the term in such contexts. In the Synoptics there is, however, not talk of 'the final dor/genea' but of 'this genea', and this phrase has there been shown to be related to a pattern of thought, which is above all to be found in the expressions 'the dor of the Flood' and 'the dor of the Wilderness'. Can this also cast light on the meaning of Jesus' statement in Mk 13:30 par. Mt 24:34, Lk 21:32?

As noticed above there are scholars who hold that the phrase has a different significance in Mk 13:30 par. than elsewhere in the synoptic Gospels. It is, however, hard to find convincing reasons for this supposition. Since the expression has such a decided character in the Synoptics that it almost has the function of a *terminus technicus*, there would have to be very good reasons for accepting that it would have a meaning in one passage which differs totally from its significance in the rest of the same group of scriptures. Such reasons have not been brought to light.

Moreover, there are positive indications that ἡ γενεὰ αὕτη in Jesus' saying has been seen from the aspect presented here. Concerning the last *genea* and its end it is primarily the typology of the *dor* of the Flood which is in focus, as the Flood was looked on as the first end of the world, which typologically foretells the last one[314]. In the ἡ γενεὰ αὕτη context in Lk 17:22-37, which is about the *parousia* and the eschatological judgement, reference is made typologically to the *dor* of the Flood and the catastrophe of the deluge and in addition to the people of Sodom and the destruction of that town, a theme which belongs to the same group of motifs.[315] As for Mt this comparison between the situation when the Flood came and what it will be like at the coming of the Son of Man, now follows immediately after Jesus' saying about ἡ γενεὰ αὕτη (and the connected words) in chap. 24:34 ff. This is a substantial indication that 'this *genea*' in the *logion* in question is seen there from the same perspective as otherwise in the Synoptics.[316] The phrase in view is not e.g. a special, isolated expression of time, the extent of which can be fixed in terms of years and decades. It is the salvation-historical situation that is in focus.[317] In that light Jesus' saying is given its significant meaning.

[314] Cf. above p.19 f., 61 and below Appendix.

[315] See above chap. 6b.

[316] That this is something completely different from the opinion that 'this *genea*' refers to mankind in general (cf. above p. 83 f.) does not need to be explained further.

[317] Cf. below chap. 10.

It is said about ἡ γενεὰ αὕτη that it "will not pass away (οὐ μὴ παρέλθῃ) until...." What then about this wording? When the verb παρέρχεσθαι 'pass away' is used in this manner about 'this *genea*', it is in complete agreement with what happened to earlier sinful *dorot/geneai* according to the Old Testament and early Jewish thought, and it gains its significance against that background. 'The *dor* of the Flood' as well as 'the *dor* of the Wilderness' were struck by God's punishments, and, as has been shown above, it is part of the picture that they were destroyed in their entirety.[318] "Not a remnant of them was left".[319] They passed away. But mankind lived on.

In contrast to this, it is said about ἡ γενεὰ αὕτη that it will not pass away until the *parousia* and the eschatalogical end take place. It is not like the '*dor* of the Flood' and 'the *dor* of the Wilderness' which were removed from the face of the earth and after which life continued. 'This *genea*' is not only one in a line of evil *dorot/geneai* which have been struck by the judgments of God. It is the '*genea*' of the fulfilment in a salvation-historical sense, on its way towards 'the second end' of the world with its radical judgment.[320]

With this signification, the *logion* in Mk 13:30 par. strongly expresses the tense eschatological situation present. That is where the stress lies. 'This *genea*' has the final judgment hanging over it. Unexpected like the Flood will it come (Mt 24:37–39; Lk 17:26 f.; cf. 1 Thess 5:2 f.). This implies an urgent admonition to the people of ἡ γενεὰ αὕτη: Repent![321] For the possibility of repentance exists until the End will come.[322] And to those who believe in the Son of Man, it is surely a word of comfort for the last evil time: they can look forward to his approaching *parousia* with hope and confidence (cf. Mk 13:20 par.; Mk 13:29 par.; Lk 21:28). But it also means an incitement to be steadfast and constantly prepared for his coming and the End – see chapter 6 above regarding Mk 8:38 and Lk 17:25 ff.[323] This is what is emphasized

---

[318] See above p. 12–16, 65.

[319] This is said of 'the *dor* of the Flood' in *Gen. Rab.* 38:6 (77b).

[320] NB that παρέρχεσθαι is the same word which is used of heaven and earth in the subsequent passage: "Heaven and earth will 'pass away', but ..."; cf. also Mt 5:18; Lk 16:17; 2 Pet 3:10. The verb has thus in the context "einen eschatologischen Klang" (J. Schneider in *TWNT* 2, 680); it contains a cosmic-universal dimension (cf. F. Mussner, *op. cit.*, 24).

[321] Cf. the preaching of repentance for 'the *dor* of the Flood', 'the *dor* of the Wilderness' etc.; see above chap. 1 and below Appendix.

[322] See above p. 37 and 80.

[323] Cf. 1QpHab 7:10–12: the hands of the men of truth who keep the Law "shall not slacken in the service of truth when the final age (הקץ האחרון) is prolonged".

in different ways in the subsequent verses of the chapter in question in all the Synoptics (Mk 13:33–37; Mt 24:37–51; Lk 21:34–36).[324]

Mk 13:30 par. having this meaning, the following word about the time for the *parousia* being unknown (v. 32 par. Mt 24:36) is of course entirely compatible with it. In its context in Mk 13 par. Mt 24 the statement is an indication that in the ἡ γενεὰ αὕτη *logion* it is not a matter of calculating dates and times but of waiting continously for the Son of Man and being ready for his coming and the end of the world.

---

[324] Concerning these passages se E. Lövestam, *Spiritual Wakefulness in the New Testament*, 1963, 78–91, 95–107, and 122–132 respectively.

9. Peter's Appeal on the Day of Pentecost

In the texts dealt with so far the phrase ἡ γενεὰ αὕτη only occurs on Jesus' lips. This is the case throughout the synoptic Gospels. Apart from the quotation in Heb 3:10 and the OT reference in Phil 2:15[325] there is only one exception from this in the entire New Testament, namely the appeal for repentance in Acts 2:40.

Peter's address to the Jews and proselytes who had gathered on the day of Pentecost, according to Luke's presentation led to them being cut to the heart and asking: "What shall we do?" (Acts 2:37). Peter urged them to repent and be baptized in the name of Jesus Christ so that their sins may be forgiven; then they would receive the gift of the holy Spirit. And Luke continues: "With many other words he pressed his case and pleaded with them, 'Save yourselves from this crooked *genea*'" (2:40).

Luke thus indicates that Peter repeated his message in words and phrases which are not given in detail.[326] But the content of what he said is expressed in his exhortation: σώθητε ἀπὸ τῆς γενεᾶς τῆς σκολιᾶς ταύτης. This appeal is a summary of Peter's pleading with his listeners. As such it has, of course, great importance and its formulation in the context here is notable. We can observe that he is speaking of being saved not from sin or death or anything similar, but from 'this crooked *genea*'.

The long quotation from Joel at the beginning of Peter's address ends in a σωθήσεται (in the absolute sense): "Everyone who invokes the name of the Lord 'will be saved'" (v. 21). It is LXX Joel 3:5a which is quoted. Joel 3:5 is also referred to in the near context of Peter's exhortation in v. 40 - confer in v. 39b the phrase ὅσους ἂν προσ-καλέσηται κύριος with LXX Joel 3:5: οὓς κύριος προσκέκληται. This supports the assumption that σώθητε in Peter's appeal is connected to σωθήσεται in the quotation from Joel in v. 21.[327] The special formulation of the appeal cannot, however, be satisfactorally explained by referring to the Joel text.[328]

---

[325] Regarding these passages see below chap. 10.

[326] NB imperf. παρεκάλει (v. 40).

[327] Gerhard Schneider, *Die Apostelgeschichte* I, 1980, 278; Gerd Lüdemann, *Das frühe Christentum*, 1987, 52 f.; and others. – ⊓⊓⊓/κύριος in Joel is assigned to Jesus in Peter's speech; see e.g. J. Roloff, *Die Apostelgeschichte*, 1982, 54 f.

[328] That is the case even if you as e.g. F.F. Bruce think you can find an affinity between

In this regard reference has been made to Ps 12:8 (LXX 11:8).[329]
There it says (LXX):... καὶ διατηρήσεις ἡμᾶς (MT וּתִּצְּרֶנּוּ) ἀπὸ τῆς
γενεᾶς ταύτης 'and you will preserve us from this *genea* (MT *dor*)'.
That is not a direct equivalent of the expression in Acts 2:40. It has,
however, been pointed out that in the Targum it says 'this *evil*
generation' and that נצר e.g. in the Samaritan Liturgy is found in the
sense 'to save, rescue'. We should then obtain: 'and thou shalt rescue
them from this evil generation', and this corresponds to the wording in
Peter's appeal. This argumentation is, however, too complicated to be
convincing.[330]

Yet there are expressions in early Jewish literature which correspond
to the formulation of Peter's appeal. Here the rabbinical comment
referred to above on Moses' changing of Joshua's name from Hoshea to
Joshua (Num 13:16) should be noted. It says: "When Moses saw that
they (i.e. the spies) were very wicked he said to him (viz.
Hoshea/Joshua): 'May God save you from this evil *dor*[331] (יהוה יושיעך מן
הדור הרע הזה)'".[332] This corresponds completely to the way of expression
in Acts 2:40.

Even if this tradition regarding the change of name is difficult to
give a date, it shows that the formulation of Peter's exhortation is
entirely within the framework of the early Jewish conception of the
dor/genea in focus here. The quoted rabbinic passage deals with the
dor of the Wilderness. In itself, it does not say so much about Peter's
pentecostal appeal. But in addition to the wording comes the fact that
the term γενεὰ σκολιά, which is used there, undoubtedly alludes to
Deut 32:5 and/or LXX Ps 77(78):8 (cf. Phil 2:15)[333] , and in both these
passages it is precisely that *dor* which is meant. It has also been seen to

a saved 'remnant' of the people in Joel and Peter's urging his hearers to save themselves
from 'this crooked *genea*' in Acts 2:40 (*The Book of the Acts*, 1954 [1972], 78 f.).
As for Joel 3:5 in this respect cf. however W. Rudolph, *Joel-Amos-Obadja-Jona*,
1971, 73 f.; H.W. Wolff, *Joel and Amos,* 1977, 68 f.

[329] Max Wilcox, *The Semitisms of Acts,* 1965, 30.

[330] Wilcox himself states, ..."while we must be quite emphatic that this case is far from
conclusive in its own right, yet nevertheless in the light of the other phenomena already
observed and noted it would seem to be at least suggestive", *op. cit.,* 30.

[331] Viz. the *dor* of the Wilderness; see above p. 16.

[332] *Tanch.* שלח 9 (33a; ed. Buber); par. *Num. Rab.* 16:9 (69a).

[333] Cf. Ernst Haenchen, *Die Apostelgeschichte,* 1977, 186; G. Schneider, *Die
Apostelgeschichte* I, 1980, 278; I.H. Marshall, *The Acts of the Apostles,* 1980, 82;
R. Maddox, *The Purpose of Luke–Acts,* 1982, 111; R. Pesch, *Die Apostelgeschichte*
I, 1986, 126.

be one of the *dorot/geneai* most referred to in Jesus' sayings about 'this *genea*' in the Synoptics. We have to see and understand Peter's words in this light .

It is then important here that judgement and punishment were intimately connected with such entities as 'the *dor* of the Flood' and 'the *dor* of the Wilderness'.[334] These *dorot* have even been named after their punishments. Belonging to the *dor*, being of the *dor*, meant that people were also subjected to its punishment. But distancing themselves from the *dor* due to faith and obedience to God and thus not belonging to it in its faithlessness and spiritual perversity meant on the other hand that they would escape the impending doom. It applies to Noah and those close to him in relation to 'the *dor* of the Flood'. It applies to people like Joshua and Caleb in relation to 'the *dor* of the Wilderness' (p.15 f.). And it applies to those who believed in Jesus in relation to the γενεά which he addresses as 'this (unbelieving and perverse) *genea*'. To be saved (with eschatalogical implications) people must repent and seperate themselves spiritually from 'this *genea*' and receive God's works of salvation sent to them through 'the second Redeemer'.

According to what is indicated inter alia by the terminology it is primarily the conception of 'the *dor* of the Wilderness' that is to be found in the background of Peter's call. In the context in Acts 2 there is a fact that gives rise to the need to emphasize even here that, according to the OT presentation, that *dor* demonstrated its lack of faith *in spite of the mighty works* for their salvation that they had witnessed. This characteristic has been seen to be of importance in ἡ γενεά αὕτη passages in the synoptic Gospels, especially in the texts of the demand for a sign (Mk 8:12; Mt 16:4; Mt 12:39–42 par. Lk 11:29–32). In those contexts Jesus consistently talks of 'this (wicked) *genea*'.[335]

In Peter's Pentecostal speech christology has a dominant place (Acts 2:22 ff.). We note that regarding Jesus' earthly appearance and deeds and the reactions against him, the presentation is completely in line with the recently mentioned pattern in the exodus texts of the Old Testament and in the Synoptics. It refers precisely to Jesus having carried out 'mighty works and wonders and signs' among the people. That this had happened in the presence of those who were Peter's audience is strongly marked: εἰς ὑμᾶς 'to you', ἐν μέσῳ ὑμῶν 'in your midst' (v. 22). And Jesus' mighty acts are seen from the perspective that Jesus was accredited by God through these deeds. Just as with Moses at 'the first exodus'[336] God had thus attested that it was he who had sent Jesus and

---

[334] See above chap. 1.

[335] Above chap. 3.

was working through him. In spite of that, Jesus had not been received but rejected and crucified. It is in the context of the speech, which describes the mission and earthly activities of Jesus in *that* way, that Peter's preaching about repentance is summarised in the saying about ἡ γενεὰ αὕτη.

That suggests that it is not just a case of a formal, terminological connection with OT texts regarding 'the *dor* of the Wilderness' but that the aspect is the same as e.g. in the gospel passages of the demand for a sign. Peter's speech had Jews and proselytes as addressees, and for Jewish listeners the occurences of the exodus were well-known. To them the wanderers in the desert were a familiar *dor*, whose behaviour served as a warning example of rebelliousness and lack of faith.

Within this frame of reference Peter's way of expression gets its significant meaning. It implies a strong emphasis of the guilt of that *genea*, who, in spite of all the mighty deeds God let Jesus carry out, rejected him and had him crucified and killed – him whom God made both Lord and Messiah (v. 36). That *genea* therefore stands under impending judgement. And if Peter's addressees are to avoid being struck by judgement like the *dor* of the Wilderness, it is necessary for them to save themselves from 'this crooked *genea*'.[337] Peter's appeal with those implications strongly reinforces the call to repent. It is most suitable as a summary of his preaching on conversion for the Jewish addressees.

Regarding the early Christian missionary activity as it is depicted in Acts and the New Testament letters, Peter's conversion terminology is unique. Taking into consideration the above results regarding the occurrence and meaning of the phrase 'this (wicked) *genea*' in the Synoptics - with its limitation to the sayings by Jesus - it is, however, hard to assume that the wording in Acts 2:40 could have come from Luke. It must be concluded that it is a matter of a prelukian tradition.[338]

---

[336] Further above p. 22.

[337] The verb in Peter's appeal is in the imper. pass., and it has rightly been pointed out that that is a form which here implies godly activity; cf. G. Stählin, *Die Apostelgeschichte*, 1962, 55.

[338] Cf. O. Bauernfeind, *Kommentar und Studien zur Apostelgeschichte*, hrsg. von V. Metelmann, (1939) 1980, p. 33, 52, 54. – When E. Haenchen means: "Lukas gliedert hier nur eine Wendung der christlichen Missionssprache ein" (*Die Apostelgeschichte*, 1977, 186), documentation is unfortunately lacking.

10. The γενεά References in Phil 2:12-16 and Heb 3:7-4:11

In the New Testament letters there are two *genea* texts of relevance in this connection, namely Phil 2:15 and Hebr 3:10. In both cases they contain Old Testament references. In the first case there is an allusion to Deut 32:5 and in the latter a quotation from Ps 95:10 (LXX 94:10). The phrase 'this *genea*' itself is only found in the quotation.

a) *Phil 2:12-16*

Phil 1:27-2:16 contains a paraenesis which includes, among other things, the Christ hymn in 2:6-11. In the hymn Jesus' obedience to death on a cross is stressed, and it is emphasized that God therefore (διό) highly exalted him and bestowed on him the name above all names, i.e. IHWH (*Kyrios*). In conjunction with this hymn (ὥστε) the Philippians are, with reference to their obedience, admonished to work out their own salvation, for it is God who is at work in them (vs. 12 f.). In the continuation, the addressees are exhorted: "Do all things without 'grumbling' and 'questioning', that you may be blameless and innocent, children of God without blemish in the midst of a crooked and perverse *genea* (μέσον γενεᾶς σκολιᾶς καὶ διεστραμμένης), among whom you shine as lights in the world..." (vs. 14–16).

It is usually and quite rightly pointed out that the saying in vs. 14 f. has been noticably influenced by the language of the Old Testament.[339] The connection with the terminology normally used in talking about Israel in the wilderness is particularly marked.

When the Philippians are exhorted to do everything without 'grumbling' and 'questioning', the Greek has the terms γογγυσμός and διαλογισμός. The prior is part of the terminology that is frequently used when speaking of the behaviour of the *dor* of the Wilderness with their opposition to Moses (and Aaron) and thus to God. In MT the Hebr. לון ('murmur') is a central term used to describe their challenges. Apart from in Josh 9:18, the verb only appears with this function in the

[339] See e.g. J. Gnilka, *Der Philipperbrief*, 1968, 151; R. Martin, *Philippians*, 1980, 104.

Hebrew Bible (Ex 15:24; 16:2,7,8; 17:3; Num 14:2,27,29,36; 16:11; 17:6,20). In all cases it is rendered in the LXX with γογγύζειν or διαγογγύζειν. Even if it does occur in the LXX that these verbs are also found in a more general sense (e.g. Is 29:24; Lam 3:39), they are used particularly of the behaviour of the people in the desert (cf. also Num 11:1; LXX Ps 105:25 [106:25]).[340] The same applies to the noun γογγυσμός, which normally stands for MT's תְּלֻנָּה (תְּלֻנּוֹת) (Ex 16:7,8,9,12; Num 17:20,25).[341]

The word διαλογισμός, '(evil) thought, anxious reflection or doubt, dispute'[342], is not, like γογγυσμός, specially tied to Israel's behaviour at the time of the first exodus in the LXX. It is clear that in its combination with the latter term in a double-expression it has a pejorative sense.[343] An element of doubt is often, with justification, sensed in the word.[344] It then captures a basic characteristic of the behaviour of the people during the wandering in the desert. When they opposed Moses (and Aaron) in the work of liberation time and time again and posed their questions and laid forth their arguments, this exposed the fundamental, underlying question of their doubts: Was the Lord among them or not? (Ex 17:7).[345]

The formulation χωρὶς γογγυσμῶν καὶ διαλογισμῶν is to be seen and understood from this perspective. In addition to the terminology, the following final clause (ἵνα...,v.15) indicates this clearly. The Philippians' Christian behaviour according to the exhortation of Paul is there given as a contrast to the attitude of a 'crooked and perverse *genea*', a phrase which is taken from LXX Deut 32:5 and which refers precisely to the *dor* of the Wilderness in that passage. Paul's warning does not then concern complaints and futile arguments among the

---

[340] Cf. the stress put on the murmurings of the *dor* of the Wilderness in 4 Ezra 1:15: "Thus says the Lord Almighty: The quails were a sign to you; I gave you camps for your protection, and in them you complained (*murmurastis*)". For the expanded form of 4 Ezra including the chapters 1-2 and 15-16, see B.M. Metzger, *The Fourth Book of Ezra* in *OTP* I, 1983, 517 f. Cf. Sir 46:7, where it is said about Moses and Caleb that they appeased 'the wicked murmuring' (γογγυσμὸν πονηρίας).

[341] More about the terminology in question in K.H. Rengstorf, γογγύζω κτλ., *TWNT* 1, 727-737.

[342] G. Schrenk, διαλέγομαι κτλ., *TWNT* 2, 97 f.

[343] Cf. W. Schenk, *Die Philipperbriefe des Paulus*, 1984, 220.

[344] See e.g. G. Schrenk, *op. cit.*, 97 f.; W. Bauer, *Wörterbuch*, 1988, s.v. Cf. E. Lohmeyer, *Der Brief and die Philipper*, 1953, 106; K.H. Rengstorf, γογγύζω κτλ., *TWNT* 1, 737 n. 7; J. Gnilka, *Der Philipperbrief*, 1968, 151 (... "hier das zweiflerische, misstrauische Bedenken").

[345] Cf. above p.14 f.

Christians at Philippi, one with another, as has sometimes been suggested.[346] Γογγυσμός and διαλογισμός are instead negatively related to the *obedience*, which is a central theme in the context (see below).

This reference to the *dor/genea* of the Wilderness brings out in relief what Paul says.

The willingness of the people to accept God's acts of salvation (through Moses) at the exodus was a matter of obedience. The weak point was disobedience. Time and time again Israel's children demonstrated this, as has been pointed out above (Ex 16:3; 17:7; Num 14:3-4,11,22; 20:10; 21:5,7; Deut 9:7,24; Ps 78:19,22; etc.). They even made themselves an idol cast in the shape of a calf (Ex 32:1 ff.), which was an extreme act of disobedience and gave rise to this complaint from the Lord: "So quickly have they turned aside from the way I commanded them" (Ex 32:8).[347] NB how in Heb 4:11 the *dor* of the Wilderness is spoken of as an example of disobedience (ὑπόδειγμα τῆς ἀπειθείας).[348]

In the context in Phil 2 obedience is also focused (cf. above). In the Christological hymn the obedience of Christ is stressed (2:8) and in relation to it, that of the Christians. In the καθώς-clause in v. 12 Paul emphasizes their demonstrated obedience, and with reference to it he calls them to work out their salvation with fear and trembling[349] (v. 12 f.). This 'work' is thus seen from the aspect of obedience.[350]

Regarding the concrete *object* of obedience it is not motivated to think primarily e.g. of the bishops and deacons mentioned earlier in the letter (chap. 1:1). In this context, Paul talks about himself in his pre-

[346] E.g. G. Hawthorne, *Philippians*, 1983, 101.

[347] Cf. LXX Num 14:43: "You turned away from the Lord in disobedience (ἀπεστράφητε ἀπειθοῦντες κυρίῳ)".

[348] Cf. Heb 3:18 ("To whom did he swear that they should never enter his rest, but to those who were disobedient [ἀπειθήσασιν]?"); 4:6 (…"those who formerly received the good news failed to enter because of disobedience [δι' ἀπείθειαν]").

[349] NB how φόβος καὶ τρόμος – a phrase with LXX background (Gen 9:2; Ex 15:16; Is 19:16; Ps 55 [54]:6; Jdt 2:28; 15:2; 4 Macc 4:10)– is connected with ὑπακοή also in 2 Cor 7:15 and Eph 6:5.

[350] Cf. H. Balz, φοβέω κτλ., *TWNT* 9, 210: "Die vorbildhafte Selbsthingabe Christi (2,8) ermöglichst für die Glaubenden keine andere Haltung als die der demütigen Hinnahme (μετὰ φόβου καὶ τρόμου) des Willens Gottes". W. Schenk (*Die Philipperbriefe des Paulus*, 1984, 215 f.) finds synonymity in the expressions used: φόβος + τρόμος "nehmen nur synonym anknüpfend nach der dazwischengeschalteten Antithese den bestimmenden Indikativ in einem Hendiadyoin auf: ὑπακοή = φόβος καὶ τρόμος".

sence and his absence respectively (2:12), and there can scarcely be any doubt that it is he who is in view. But it is, of course, not Paul as a private person that is meant. The OT exodus presentations may be of interest on this point too. The negative reactions of the people, their murmurings, were normally directed specifically towards Moses (and Aaron). But in fact not towards him as a person but as the instrument of God – sometimes the formulation is used that the people turned 'against God and against Moses' (e.g. Num 21:5,7). It was the Lord himself in his acts of salvation that they were really opposed to. In the words of Moses: "What are we? You are not murmuring against us, but against the Lord" (Ex 16:8). In a corresponding way it is Paul as the messenger of God and representative of the gospel that is to be given obedience (cf. 1:5,7,12,27; 3:17; 4:9). It is, in reality, a matter of obedience to God and the divine revelation.[351]

When Paul in what follows gives the goal for the Philippians' lives in the power of God and in obedience to him (v. 15), he is referring in a converse way to a passage in the Song of Moses in Deut 32.[352] There it is pointed out in v. 4 that the Lord is a faithful God who does no wrong, righteous and true is he. In the following verse the people of the desert wandering are contrasted to this. This obscure MT-text[353] is given in the LXX as follows: ἡμάρτοσαν οὐκ αὐτῷ τέκνα μωμητά, γενεὰ σκολιὰ καὶ διεσετραμμένη[354] (v. 5; cf. v. 20). Paul relates to this by stating the goal for the addressees that they - in contrast to the *dor/genea* of the Wilderness - be blameless and above reproach, τέκνα θεοῦ ἄμωμα ('faultless children of God'). And while Israel in the desert was γενεὰ σκολιὰ καὶ διεστραμμένη ('a crooked and perverse *genea*'), the Christians in Philippi cannot be categorised as such. As 'saints in Christ Jesus' (Phil 1:1) they have a different spirit (cf. Num 14:24). But they have to live as believers in Christ in the midst of such a *genea*.

Paul thus describes the obedient behaviour expected of the Phi-

---

[351] The experience of persecution and suffering (cf. 1:27-30) may have contributed to the appearance of conduct among the Philippians, which can have motivated the warning in question. In the wilderness it was mostly difficult experiences of different kinds - e.g. lack of food and water - which provoked the complaints.

[352] Cf. above p. 47.

[353] See e.g. A.D.H. Mayes, *Deuteronomy*, 1979 (1987), 383; I. Drazin, *Targum Onkelos to Deuteronomy*, 1982, 271; B. Grossfeld, *The Targum Onqelos to Deuteronomy* (The Aramaic Bible 9), 1988, 90.

[354] In *The Septuagint Version of the Old Testament* (London: Bagster and Sons) the phrase is translated: "They have sinned, not /pleasing/ him; spotted children, a forward and perverse generation".

lippians against the gloomy background of the *dor* of the Wilderness with its impending punishment. Functionally it is the same as in 1 Cor 10, where he says that what happened to the desert wanderers happened τυπικῶς ('as *typos*'), and was written down as a warning for the Christian community, where he immediately prior to this mentioned the γογγυσμός among the Israelites in the desert (1 Cor 10:10 f.). The typological bringing to the fore of the faithless people of the first exodus with their well-known fate is an extra incentive for the addressees to obey Paul's admonitions to them to carry out the will of God in their lives.

In the passage there is also another feature of the same theme. In the saying that the Philippians shall become faultless children of God 'in the midst of a crooked and perverse *genea*' (v. 15) a dynamic contrast is marked. The aspect is doubtless the same as in Mk 8:38, when Jesus pronounces judgement on the one who is ashamed of him and his words 'in this adulterous and sinful *genea*'.[355] For people who are of a different spirit it involves difficulties, trials and temptations to live according to God's will in an evil and faithless *dor/genea*. Paul's way of expressing himself should be seen in this light too. It implies an exhortation to the Philippians to be steadfast in faith in spite of all the opposition, the attacks and all their suffering for the sake of Christ (Phil 1:27-30). At the same time the aspect of a possible influence on the people of the *genea* in question is apparently to be found.[356] That is indicated by the imagery of the Christians at Philippi as shining among them like lights in the world, holding fast the word of life (vs. 15 f.).

From the aspect of the *genea* terminology, the text in question has its evident interest. When Jesus in the synoptic Gospels speaks of 'this *genea*' he is addressing his Jewish surroundings. As has been shown above, however, the *dor/genea* concept in question is not defined in its content or scope by quantitative criteria but by qualitative, salvation-historical ones. Nor is there in the *dor / genea* typology itself any limitation to Israel. 'The *dor* of the Wilderness' was certainly an un-faithful *dor* of Israel. But 'the *dor* of the Flood' had a universal character.

Israel was God's chosen people. But Jesus' acts of salvation, according to early Christain belief and preaching were not intended only for Israel but for the world as a whole. As the characteristic of ἡ γενεὰ αὕτη was their attitude of rejection towards him, the Old Testament *dor/genea* terminology in its typological use was apparently seen as

---

[355] Above chap. 6a.

[356] Cf. below Appendix regarding Noah and the *dor* of the Flood.

applicable not only to the Israel of fulfilment but also, in a wider sense, to the people who have been reached by the message about him but have despised it and rejected it. It can be seen in Phil 2:15, when Paul - earlier a rabbi disciple[357] - there uses typologically the phrase γενεὰ σκολιὰ καὶ διεστραμμένη from Deut 32:5 about the unbelieving world among whom the Philippians lived without any restrictions. This corresponds to the general use of the exodus-typology on the situation of the Christian congregation in 1 Cor 10:1-11.

b) *Heb 3:7-4:11*

Following the comparison of Jesus with Moses in Heb 3:1-6, the section 3:7-4:11 deals with the situation of the believers in Christ, giving warning comparisons with the Israel of the desert wandering. The author bases his writing on Ps 95:7b–11 (LXX Ps 94:7b–11), which he quotes at length, and he interprets the text in a manner similar to the Qumranian pesher-method.[358] In his application of the Psalm passage to the Christians he urges them to be careful that they should not – like the *dor/genea* of the Wilderness – be found to have fallen short of God's rest, stressing that there assuredly remains a sabbath rest for the people of God.

Heb's quotation of the Psalm text largely follows the LXX. This also applies as regards the proper names Meribah[359] and Massah in MT (Ps 95:8; cf. Ex 17:7; Num 20:13,24; 27:14; Deut 6:16; 9:22; 32:51; 33:8; Ps 81:8; 106:32), which are in LXX Ps 94:8 rendered appellatively by παραπικρασμός (ἐν τῷ παραπικρασμῷ 'in the rebellion') and πειρασμός (κατὰ τὴν ἡμέραν τοῦ πειρασμοῦ 'on the day of testing') respectively (cf. also *Tg. Ps.*95:8).[360] This is thus not specific to Heb. There are a few differences in relation to LXX, however, which should be noted here.[361]

---

[357] The passage in question is without doubt Pauline; cf. J. Gnilka, *Der Philipperbrief*, 1968, 5–11; R. Martin, *Philippians*, 1980, 10–22; W.G. Kümmel, *Einleitung in das Neue Testament*, 1983, 291–294.

[358] Cf. B. Gärtner, "The Habakkuk Commentary (DSH) and the Gospel of Matthew", *ST* 8, 1954, 13; H. Braun, *Qumran und das Neue Testament* I, 1966, 250.

[359] For the terminology see E. Lövestam, *Spiritus blasphemia*, 1968, 18–22.

[360] See H. Braun, *An die Hebräer*, 1984, 87, where also the LXX- and *Tg.*-material on other Massah and Meribah passages in MT is discussed.

[361] Cf. moreover J.C. McCullough, "The Old Testament Quotations in Hebrews", *NTS* 26, 1980, 369–372.

One is the reference to the 'forty years'. In Heb 3:9 f. it is attached to the preceding statement and thus designates the time the fathers saw God's works, while in the LXX (as well as in MT) they are the time that God 'loathed that *dor/genea*'. The author has, of course, known of the latter reference. This is clear as he uses it himself further on in the section (3:17).[362] The question is why he then renders[363] the text as in the given quotation.[364]

As can be seen above, the mighty works, the signs and miracles that the people of the first exodus experienced are emphasized both in the Old Testament, in early Jewish literature and in the New Testament.[365] In this case it should be noted that it is stressed shortly before in Heb that the Christian salvation was manifested in signs and miracles. These are furthermore described as God's testification: "God added his testimony... by signs, by wonders, by manifold works of power" (Heb 2:4). This is in all probability the background against which we have to see the author's rearrangement of the quotation. In a more expressive way than is given in the text of MT and the LXX it emphasizes the fact that Israel in the wilderness witnessed God's mighty deeds during their wandering. As the reader has been reminded briefly before that people in the Christian community experienced God's signs and miracles and mighty works, the formulation of the quotation means a special marking of the similarities in the situation of the people of the first exodus and those of the second one. This has a concrete bearing for the receivers of the letter. Although the wanderers in the desert had certainly seen God's deeds of salvation (τὰ ἔργα μου), they had still challenged him, with their tragic fate as a result.[366] The Christian addressees are in a similar way also in danger of – in spite of their exceptional experiences of the salvation in the time of fulfilment – becoming unbelievers and turning away from the living God. In the author's quotation and its application

---

[362] Both those strands have Old Testament grounds. In the OT presentations it speaks of forty years during which Israel experienced God's mighty works and his provision (e.g. Ex 16:35: Deut 2:7; Neh 9:21), but on the other hand OT texts also speak of forty years of wrath (e.g. Num 14:33–34; 32:13); cf. W.L. Lane, *Hebrews 1–8*, 1991, 89.

[363] Such an interpretative rendering is in agreement with the ancient Jewish and early Christian view of the Scripture; cf. E. Lövestam, "Urkyrkans skriftförståelse" in *Axplock*, 1987, 17–25 (with ref.).

[364] For the discussions of this point in Heb's text, see e.g. O. Hofius, *Katapausis*, 1970, 128–130; G.W. Buchanan, *To the Hebrews*, 1972, 62; H.W. Attridge, *The Epistle to the Hebrews*, 1989, 115; E. Grässer, *An die Hebräer* I, 1990, 176; H.-F. Weiss, *Der Brief an die Hebräer*, 1991, 259–260.

[365] Above chap. 3 and 9.

[366] For the meaning of 'though they saw...' in καὶ εἶδον see e.g. E. Grässer, *op. cit.*, 179; H.-F. Weiss, *op. cit.*, 259.

to the addressees lies an extra warning to them in that respect.

Another difference between the Heb-text and the LXX that we should note in this context is that LXX's τῇ γενεᾷ ἐκείνῃ according to the best mss in Heb 3:10 is rendered τῇ γενεᾷ ταύτῃ. Is this due to a variant LXX text?[367] Or to the wish to have a more direct link to the previous clause?[368] Now the ἡ γενεὰ αὕτη terminology has been firmly established in the synoptic traditions. To all appearances it is in this light we are to see the rendering of the term in question in this case. It is then not only a matter of a stylistic change.[369] The phrase has given associations to the sayings of Jesus which made the warning application of the Psalm text to the Christian congregation still more vivid.

As regards the דור המדבר typology in its entirety it plays a basic role in Heb 3:7-4:11. In accordance with the closing words of the Psalm quotation – ..."they shall never enter my rest" (3:11) – it is the prevented entrance into Canaan that is in focus. As has been seen above, דור המדבר was looked on in ancient Israel as a totality – NB the marking of the wholeness trait in Num 14:2,5,7,19,22; Heb 3:16. The aspect of wandering in the desert does not play a central role, although it is implied in some ways. It has justly been pointed out that there is no actual reference to the people of Israel as wanderers, nor to the Christians in such terms, but that "the setting and overall thrust of the passage (the implied wanderings of Israel, the goal set but not yet realized) support at least the idea of *movement towards a goal*".[370] And the goal was the Promised Land/God's rest, the entrance into which the *dor* of the Wilderness were refused. It should be seen in that light, when in the comments on and the application of the quotation in question in Heb 3:12 ff. there are in particular references to the presentation in Num 14, where God's judgement is passed after the infidelity of the spies and the subsequent disobedience of the people.[371]

There were, however, some who reached the Land of Canaan. This applied to people like Joshua and Caleb (Num 14:6 ff.,24,30,38) and the younger ones among the desert wanderers (Num 14:29-31). The question might then be asked if the promise that they would enter the land

---

[367] Cf. H.W. Attridge, *op. cit.*, 115 f.

[368] Cf. E. Grässer, *op. cit.*, 176.

[369] As suggested by J.C. McCullough, *op. cit.*, 371.

[370] W. G. Johnsson, "The Pilgrimage Motif in the Book of Hebrews", *JBL* 97, 1978, 240.

[371] Cf. the rabbinic reference to Num 14:35 for God's judgement on the *dor* of the Wilderness (e.g. *m. Sanh.* 10:3). As to the references to Num 14 in the section in question in Heb see e.g. H.W. Attridge, *op. cit.*, 114 ff.

and the rest was not fulfilled in their case. A passage such as Josh 21:43-45 might spring to mind in this context: "The Lord gave them rest (LXX: κατέπαυσεν; cf. Heb 3:11,18; 4:1,3,5,10,11: κατάπαυσις) on every side, just as he had sworn to their fathers" (v. 44).

Here it should be noted that the warning *typos* in the Heb text is דור המדבר (3:10), and it has been shown above that those who had 'a different spirit' within them were not counted to 'the *dor* of the Wilderness' with its impending judgement.[372] Of דור המדבר no remnant was left. None of them entered the Promised Land.

But otherwise? In Heb God's rest is given a deeper dimension in reference to the creation, about which it is said that on the seventh day God 'rested' (LXX: κατέπαυσεν) from all his works (Gen 2:2; Heb 4:4; 4:9-10).[373] It is then not only a matter of the entry into Canaan and the situation there, but this is a *typos*[374] of the divine rest in a deeper and wider meaning as a heavenly reality, as "den Zielort der Verheissung Gottes als den Ort des eschatologischen Heils".[375] The author's reasoning in this context is this: If Joshua had 'given them rest' in the sense intended in the Psalm passage, would God not have again set a certain day through David much later and exhorted the people considering their entry into his rest: "Today if you hear his voice, do not harden your hearts..." The conclusion is that there remains a sabbath rest for the people of God. The addressees are then exhorted to make every effort to enter it, so that no one may fail by following the evil example of unbelief found in 'this *genea*' in the desert (4:11). That is the message of the author.

In Heb 3:7–4:11 the דור המדבר typology has thus a central place. The passage is a significant exponent of that typology in the New Testament letters (cf. 1 Cor 10:1–11). The *dor/genea* of the Wilderness with its character and behaviour and fate is brought forward to the Christian community as a warning not to let themselves be marked by the same faithlessness and disobedience as that *genea* and thus be refused entry into God's rest. This does not concern days and years. It is a question of the salvation-historical situation of the eschatological people of God on

---

[372] Above p. 15 f.

[373] The author here uses the rabbinical *gezera shawa* argument, in which a term in one verse of Scripture is interpreted according to its use in another; cf. H.W. Attridge, *The Epistle to the Hebrews*, 1989, 128 f., with references.

[374] Cf. D. Hagner, *Hebrews*, 1983, 54: "It is clear that our author sees a typological relationship between rest in the land of Canaan and the rest that God intends for Christians".

[375] H.-F. Weiss, *op. cit.*, 268. As regards 'the rest' in Heb 3:7-4:11 see e.g. O. Hofius, *Katapausis*, 1970, passim; H. Braun, *An die Hebräer*, 1984, 90–93; H.W. Attridge, *op. cit.*, 126–128; H.-F. Weiss, *op. cit.*, 268–273.

their way towards the coming sabbath rest.

It has been noted above that the *genea* terminology, which appears in the Psalm quotation, is not used in the pesher-like application in Heb. But when LXX's ἡ γενεὰ ἐκείνη is there replaced by ἡ γενεὰ αὕτη it is in all probability due to the way of expression in Jesus' teaching in the synoptic traditions. It then mirrors an associative connection with this which shows the living establishment of the ἡ γενεὰ αὕτη concept of Jesus' sayings in the early Christian world of thought.

11. Epilogue

It is characteristic of the 'this *genea*' terminology in the New Testament that it is almost entirely to be found only in the synoptic Gospels[376] and there exclusively on the lips of Jesus.[377] It is thus firmly established in the early Christian traditions as an expression used by Jesus and related to his preaching. Linguistically the Greek phrase is also to be traced back to Semitic origins.[378] And the content has been shown to have a strong Old Testament/Jewish connection. All the evidence regarding this terminology suggests that we are confronted with a genuine tradition in the sense that Jesus used this term about those to whom he addressed his message and in the midst of whom he did his mighty works, but who repulsed and rejected him.

If this is the case, the question is near to hand whether this mode of expression can disclose something about Jesus' perception of himself and his mission. Can the terminology tell us anything as regards the much discussed problem of his self-understanding?[379] In light of the above evidence about the background and the implications of the phrase, the answer must be in the affirmative.

Concerning the question of how Jesus looked on himself and his task the scholars have justly found it hazardous to base their suppositions on the epithets that are used about him in the Gospels: 'the Son of God', 'the Son of Man' etc. There are divided opinions regarding these 'titles' and their origin and historical authenticity as well as, in many cases, their specific meaning in a given context. Nor do we have access to any material which exposes Jesus' own spiritual life, giving us a glimpse of

---

[376] For the exception in Acts 2:40 and Old Testament references in Phil 2:15 and Heb 3:10) see above chap. 9 and 10.

[377] The situation is comparable in that respect with that regarding the designation 'Son of Man', which besides in the words of Jesus in the Gospels (incl. John) is also to be found only in a passage in Acts, namely in chap. 7:56.

[378] Above p. 8.

[379] About this question see e.g. F. Mussner, "Wege zum Selbstbewusstsein Jesu", *BZ* NF 12, 1968, 161–172; H.K. McArthur, *In Search of the Historical Jesus*, 1969; J. Jeremias. *Neutestamentliche Theologie* I, 1971, 239–284; R. Pesch, "Über die Autorität Jesu", *Die Kirche des Anfangs* (FS H. Schürmann), 1977, 25–55; T. Holtz, *Jesus aus Nazareth*, 1979, 84–94; W. Kasper, *Jesus der Christus*, 1981, 112–126; R. Leivestad, *Hvem ville Jesus være?* 1982; James H. Charlesworth, *Jesus within Judaism*, 1989, 131–164; W.G. Kümmel, "Jesusforschung seit 1981. V. Der persönliche Anspruch sowie der Prozess und Kreuzestod Jesu", *TRu* 56, 1991, 391–420.

his thoughts and feelings. Instead we must start from the presentations of his words and deeds that we find in the texts. His identity appears in what he does and says. In that context the terminology in question, with the signification which has become apparent here, is important.

In the New Testament ἡ γενεὰ αὕτη is seen from the salvation-historical aspect. 'This *genea*' is characterised by having experienced God's works of salvation at the time of fulfilment but reacting with doubt, disbelief and rejection. The salvation-historical character is underlined, among other ways, by the fact that in the Gospels the phrase can be related not only to the rejection of the Son of Man but also to the repudiation of the forerunner[380] and of the messengers sent out by Jesus.[381]

But in the centre is Jesus and his message and deeds. A study of the material has shown that the term in question with its negative tone almost always occurs in contexts which deal with the people's doubting and repudiating attitudes to him, the Son of Man: in the parable of the children in the market-place (Mt 11:16 ff. par. Lk 7:31 ff.), in the texts of the demand for a sign (Mk 8:11 ff.; Mt 16:1 ff.; 12:39 ff. par. Lk 11:16,29 ff.) etc.[382] It is he and God's work of salvation through him that are in focus. The negative qualification of the phrase is based on the people's rejection of him due to their unbelief. And it is this attitude to him that prompts his judgement on 'this *genea*'.

This says something vital about Jesus' self-understanding. When he used the ἡ γενεὰ αὕτη terminology with the meaning that has been established here, he evidently perceived himself to be 'the second Redeemer' in a typological and eschatological perpective. He regarded himself as the Saviour sent by God according to the promises of the Scriptures, as the one to whom the prophesied salvation at the end of time is related. And this in such a decisive way that the final fate of mankind – salvation or judgement (e.g. Mt 12:41 f. par.) – depends on their attitude towards him.

---

[380] See above chap. 4.

[381] Chap. 7 above.

[382] See further above p. 19.

APPENDIX

The Argumentation against the Scoffers
in 2 Pet 3:3–13[383]

In 2 Pet the eschatalogical question has a predominent place.[384] In his counter-argument to the scoffers'[385] mocking denial of the hope of Christ's return, the author treats the theme fairly broadly in chap. 3:3-13. He presents a number of arguments for the end of the world and the *parousia*. An analysis of his argumentation shows that he, to a large extent, uses conceptions that we find in the ancient Jewish world of ideas. How should this be understood? Has the author used Jewish ways of thought for his own purpose without giving them a Christian re-interpretation?[386] Has he, in a desparate situation, grasped at different Jewish notions and motifs and coordinated those *ad hoc*?[387] Does his presentation contain a disparate collection of different arguments, which in fact show his confusion when faced with the early Christian apocalyptic?[388] What is the true situation regarding his roots in genuine

---

[383] In this section the *dor/genea* terminology itself is not to be found.

[384] It is certainly not first introduced in chap. 3; cf. T. Fornberg, *An Early Church in a Pluralistic Society*, 1977, 40–47; 78–93; J.H. Neyrey, "The Form and Background of the Polemic in 2 Peter", *JBL* 99, 1980, 407–431; J. Kahmann, "The Second Letter of Peter and the Letter of Jude. Their Mutual Relationship", *The New Testament in Early Christianity* (BETL 86), 1989, 105–121.

[385] It is difficult to identify the heretics in 2 Pet with any certainty. They are often said to be proponents of a false doctrine of a gnostic or incipient gnostic type; for ref. see R.J. Bauckham, "2 Peter: An Account of Research", *ANRW* II,25:5, 1988, 3724 f. This can not be shown convincingly in the text in question; cf. Fornberg, *op. cit.*, 70; Klaus Berger, "Streit um Gottes Vorsehung. Zur Position der Gegner im 2. Petrusbrief", *Tradition and Re-interpretation in Jewish and Early Christian Literature* (FS J. Lebram), 1986, 121-135. See further in this matter e.g. R.J. Bauckham, *op. cit.*, 3724–3728; J. Kahmann, *op. cit.*, 114–121. H. Paulsen comes to the conclusion that the scoffers in 3:3 f. should not be categorised as a particular group of opponents and states: "Es ist vielmehr deutlich, dass der Vf. ein grundsätzliches Problem des frühen Christentums und seiner Theologie mit traditionellen Argumenten und Erwägungen beantworten will" (*Der Zweite Petrusbrief und der Judasbrief*, 1992, 157).

[386] Cf. D. von Allmen, "L'apocalyptique juive et le retard de la parousie en II Pierre 3:1–13", *RTP* 16, 1966, 268 f.

[387] Cf. W. Harnisch, *Eschatologische Existenz* , 1973, 104.

Christian faith?[389]

This problem complex raises the question as to whether there is, in the author's many-facetted argumentation, any fundamental element which gives coherence to the different points of his apologia. And if this is the case, how does this perspective connect backwards to the early Christian tradition?[390]

The dissidents ask contemptuously: "Where is the promise of his coming?" They point out that all things have continued as they were from the beginning of creation (3:4). By this they mean that everything will also continue as it has been. There is no *parousia* and no final judgement to be expected.[391]

The Flood is here brought into the author's counter argument. The Creator is supreme in relation to the world he has created, something which he demonstrated in the catastrophe of the Flood (3:5-6). The reference to the Flood is given special weight through the typological perspective in ancient Judaism and early Christianity, according to which the Flood was seen as 'the first consummation', to which 'the eternal judgment' corresponds (e.g. *1 Enoch* 93:1–10, 91:12–17).[392] They were also familiar with the idea, that while 'the first end' came by water, the second, eschatalogical end would come by fire.[393] Within the framework of this view was the fact that the prototype had actually taken place providing a guarantee that its typological counterpart would also come about.[394]

---

[388] Cf. Siegfried Schulz, *Die Mitte der Schrift*, 1976, 301.

[389] Regarding its accord with early Christian eschatology the apologia in 2 Pet 3:3 ff. is the object of a strongly critical evaluation by E. Käsemann ("Eine Apologie der urchristlichen Eschatologie", ZTK 49, 1952, 272–296), D. von Allmen (*op. cit.*, 255–274) et al., while others are more positive, e.g. K.H. Schelkle (*Die Petrusbriefe. Der Judasbrief*, 1961, 245); T. Fornberg (*op. cit.*, 91, 148); Anton Vögtle (*Der Judasbrief / Der zweite Petrusbrief*, 1994, 272–278).

[390] Cf. E. Lövestam, "Eschatologie und Tradition im 2. Petrusbrief", *The New Testament Age* (FS Bo Reicke) II, 1984, 287-300.

[391] A. Vögtle rightly points out : "Mit dieser Behauptung setzen sie selbstverständlich den Fortbestand des Universums mit der Erde als Ort des geschichtlichen Geschehens voraus, was sie aber keineswegs zugleich mit der prinzipiellen Unzerstörbarkeit des Universums begründet haben mussten" (*op. cit.*, 221).

[392] See above p. 19 f. with ref.

[393] *Vita Adae et Evae* 49:3. For the Dead Sea scriptures cf. A. Vögtle, *Das Neue Testament und die Zukunft des Kosmos*, 1970, 133. Regarding the conception of an eschatalogical world fire see above all R. Mayer, *Die biblische Vorstellung vom Weltbrand*, 1956. Cf. R. Bauckham, *Jude, 2 Peter*, 1983, 298-301; H. Paulsen, *op. cit.*, 162 f.

[394] Regarding the task of the historical references to confirm that God's judgement would fall on sinners see e.g. J. Schlosser, "Les jours de Noé et de Lot. A propos de

An essential factor in this context is now the conception of 'the *dor* of the Flood' dealt with above. The people in view in the author's argumentation lived before the coming eschatalogical judgement. Their situation was thus comparable in a typological sense to that of דור המבול. It then becomes important to focus on that concept with the complexity of ideas that were associated with it and study the author's exposition in this light.

This is further motivated by the way of presentation used previously in the letter. As has been noted earlier, 'the *dor* of the Flood' is often mentioned in ancient Jewish literature in combination with certain other *dorot* or collectives in history: 'Enoch's *dor*', 'the *dor* of the Dispersion', 'the men of Sodom', 'the *dor* of the Wilderness' etc.[395] All these have in common that they showed themselves to be disobedient to God and, in their unrighteousness and evil state, were struck by God's judgement. Against this background the author's comments in chap. 2:4 ff. come within our sphere of interest. This passage has a parallel in Jude vs. 5–7.[396] When the idea of the impending doom is brought into the narration there, reference is made - as typological examples[397] - to the *dor* of the Wilderness, to the fallen angels and to Sodom and Gomorrah and the surrounding cities. There is a similar argumentation in 2 Pet 2:4–8, here, however, with references to the judgement that struck the wicked angels[398], the *dor* of the Flood and Sodom and

---

Luc, XVII, 26–30", *RB* 80, 1973, 13–36. Cf. S. Meier, "2 Peter 3,3-7 – An Early Jewish and Christian Response to Eschatological Skepticism", *BZ* 32, 1988, 255–257.

[395] See above p. 11.

[396] As regards the relation between 2 Pet and Jud the vast majority of scholars hold that 2 Peter is dependent on Jude; cf. R. Bauckham, "2 Peter: An Account of Research", *ANRW* II,25:5, 1988, 3714–3716 (with ref.); J. Kahmann, *op. cit.*, 106–113; H. Paulsen, *op. cit.*, 97–100; A. Vögtle, *Der Judasbrief / Der zweite Petrusbrief*, 1994, 122 f.

[397] Cf. J.A. Loader, *A Tale of Two Cities*, 1990, 123.

[398] On the question of the fallen angels see e.g. F. Dexinger, *Sturz der Göttersöhne oder Engel vor der Sintflut?* 1966; T. Fornberg, *An Early Church in a Pluralistic Society*, 1977, 50–53; E. Fuchs–P. Reymond, *La deuxième épitre de Saint Pierre. L' épitre de Saint Jude*, 1980, 164; J.A. Loader, *op. cit.*, 122–124; J. Daryl Charles, "Jude's Use of Pseudepigraphical Source-Material as Part of a Literary Strategy", *NTS* 37, 1991, 134-137. - When in 2 Pet 2:4-5, after the reference to the sin of the angels and their punishment, note is made of the catastrophe of the Flood and what happened then, it should be noticed that in ancient Jewish scriptures it is common that the wickedness which provoked the punishment of the Flood is traced back to the fall of the 'sons of God' and its consequences (Gen 6:2 ff.); cf. *1 Enoch* 6:1–10:2; CD 2:17–21; *T. Naph.* 3:5; *Tg. Neof. Gen.* 6:2–3 et al. In *T. Naph.* 3:4-5 the reference to the Watchers (i.e. the angels; cf. *Jub.* 4:15) is preceded by a reference to Sodom, which also departed from the order of nature.

Gomorrah. In this case the examples referred to are presented in the correct chronological order. Of special interest to us is that, in contrast to the text in Jude, the reference to the *dor* of the Wilderness is lacking in 2 Pet, while a reference to the *dor* of the Flood has been introduced instead.

This combination of *dorot* and collectives shows that the author's argumentation in 2 Pet 3:3-13 moves within the above mentioned field of thought. Seen within the framework of the composition of 2 Pet it is likely that the specific reference to the *dor* of the Flood has been made primarily with the exposition in chap. 3 in view. The same applies to the stress on the fact that the godly were rescued - Noah and his closest family (2 Pet 2:5), Lot (2:7) - something which also distinguishes 2 Pet from Jude.

What is the result of a closer analysis of 2 Pet 3:3-13 against this background?

To start with, the very point of departure in 2 Pet shows considerable similarity to the situation before the Flood according to ancient Jewish picture. The people of דור המבול turned their backs on God and lived according to their own desires. They did not listen to the warnings from the righteous Noah.[399] His exhortations fall on deaf ears.[400] The people turned against him instead.[401] In some passages in early Jewish literature it is also said that people used ridicule as a weapon (cf. 2 Pet 3:4). They called Noah a 'contemptible old man' (*Gen. Rab.* 30:7 [62b]), they sneered at him, 'calling him demented, a man gone mad' (*Sib. Or.* I, 171 f.[402]) etc. In their heedless sense of security and their scornful ignoral of the danger of impending doom, the heretics in 2 Pet show a clear affinity to the *dor* of the Flood.

In both cases the unbelievers are also on their way towards judgement. This has not the character of individual retribution in the sense that it only affects a number of different people who have left the path of righteousness. It is rather a matter of a cosmic catastrophe

---

[399] As regards Noah's righteousness cf. above p. 12–14. Regarding Noah as a preacher see 2 Pet 2:5; cf. Jack P. Lewis, *A Study of the Interpretation of Noah and the Flood in Jewish and Christian Literature*, 1968, 37, 102 (with ref.); J. Schlosser, *op. cit.*, 32 (with ref.); D. Hagner, *The Use of the Old and New Testaments in Clement of Rome*, 1973, 247.

[400] Noah spoke "in vain to a lawless *genea*", as it is formulated in *Sib. Or.* I, 199.

[401] Josephus, *Ant* I,3:1 § 74; *Lev. Rab.* 27:5 (39b); *Eccles. Rab.* 3:15 (11b) et al. Cf. above p. 62.

[402] *Sib. Or.* I, 1–323 contains part of an original Jewish oracle, which in the judgement of J.J. Collins "probably carried its review of history no later than the time of Augustus, and so the dating suggested by Kurfess, about the turn of the era, is most likely correct" ("Sibylline Oracles", *OTP* I, 1983, 331).

which is going to strike creation. On this point the typological reference to the punishment of the *dor* of the Flood is, as has been mentioned, clearly expressed in 2 Pet. It does also occur in Jewish texts that the catastrophe of the deluge is depicted in eschatalogically coloured terms, which makes this parallelism even more striking (e.g. *1 Enoch* 83:3 f.).[403]

Just as before the Flood – the first end of the world – according to 2 Pet the *dor/genea* in general are going towards a waiting catastrophe of judgement at the second, eschatological end. All who have not accepted salvation are on the way towards ἀπώλεια (3:7b). Just as Noah in his situation preached repentance, so also in 2 Pet μετάνοια is the alternative to ἀπώλεια (v. 9). People must repent to avoid the impending doom.

That God wants the repentance and salvation of *all* (v. 9b) is a notion that is well documented in relevant literature.[404] In this context there is reason to note that this sometimes occurs in connection with Noah's preaching. In *Sib. Or.* I, 128 f. Noah is thus given the task of preaching (κηρύσσειν; cf. 2 Pet 2:5, where Noah is designated δικαιοσύνης κῆρυξ) repentance "to all the peoples, so that all may be saved" (ὅπως σωθῶσιν ἅπαντες).

Reference to the promise of the new heavens and the new earth (Is 65:17[405]; cf. 66:22) is also in accordance with the Flood typology. It is a recurring conception in the ancient Jewish and early Christian world of thought that there followed a new beginning after 'the first consummation'. Those who survived the deluge introduced 'a second cycle of time' (δευτέρα περίοδος; Philo, *Vita Mosis* 2:65). It became 'a second age' (δεύτερος αἰών; *Or. Sib.* I,195). In *1 Clem.* Noah is said, in his service, to have preached 'a rebirth to the world' (παλιγγενεσία κόσμῳ; 9:4)[406], etc. It is a case of radical renewal. In this persepctive a Flood typological application is given to the *eschaton*, as in e.g. *1 Enoch* 10:16-11:2. As L. Hartman puts it: "Noah is regarded as the 'type' of all the righteous, the flood is seen as prefiguring the judgement, and Noah's escape and behaviour after the flood stand for the

---

[403] Cf. L. Goppelt, *Typos. Die typologische Deutung des Alten Testaments im Neuen*, 1939, 38.

[404] Ezek 18:23; Wis 11:23–26; 1 Tim 2:4 etc. Rabbinical evidence in Str-B 3, 774 f.

[405] This text has given rise to a considerable 'Wirkungsgeschichte' in Jewish theology; cf. H. Paulsen, *op. cit.*, 170 f.

[406] *1 Clem.* has the same Flood typological type of argumentation as 2 Pet; cf. Otto Knoch, *Eigenart und Bedeutung der Eschatologie im theologischen Aufriss des ersten Clemensbriefes*, 1964, 211, 298.

eschatalogical salvation and bliss of the righteous people".[407] And in this world of the *eschaton* righteousness will reign (cf. 2 Pet 3:13). This is strongly emphasized: the plant of righteousness and truth will appear forever (10:16), all the righteous shall escape and they will be alive until they beget thousands (10:17), all the earth will be tilled in righteousness (10:18), all the children of the people will become righteous (10:21).[408] After 'the first consummation', according to this way of thinking, a rebirth took place, which typologically forboded the radical new creation in the sign of righteousness after the eschatological end of the world.[409]

It can thus be seen that the presentation in 2 Pet 3:3-13 moves in a motif and conceptual sphere which was related to the *dor* of the Flood and the catastrophe of the deluge. The central problem in the passage is, however, the *delay of the parousia*. The question is how the author's argumentation on this decisive point agrees with the דור המבול perspective and how it appears in this light.

With reference to Ps 90:4 the author first reminds the reader that according to the Scriptures God's measure of time is totally different from our own (v. 8).[410] The chronological calculations and speculations regarding the *parousia* and the end of the world are thus of no value. Everything is in God's hands.[411]

Then he relates more directly to the question brought to the fore by the heretics, and states: οὐ βραδύνει κύριος τῆς ἐπαγγελίας (3:9a). In the verb βραδύνειν c.gen. lies here not only the thought of a delay, pure and simple, but a delay which has as a consequence that the

---

[407] Lars Hartman, "An early example of Jewish exegesis: 1 Enoch 10:16–11:2", *Neot* 17, 1983, 20.

[408] Hartman shows how the author bases his description of the *eschaton* on the Noah story and wishes, probably quite rightly, to place the emphasis on righteousness in connection with the fact that Noah is regarded as the 'type' of all the righteous (*op. cit.*, 19-22). Cf. how Noah in 2 Pet 2:5 is described as 'a herald of righteousness'. A few verses later God is said to have rescued 'righteous Lot'.

[409] NB A. Vögtle's comment: "Auch dort, wo nachkanonisch das Verständnis der Sintflut als Weltuntergang auftaucht, wird über das Dass und Wie einer nachfolgenden Neuschöpfung nicht direkt reflektiert... Im Interesse seiner typologischen Relation zwischen der einstigen Zerstörung der geordneten Welt durch Wasser und der kommenden durch Feuer muss unser Vf. der 'damaligen Welt' freilich 'die jetzigen Himmel und die (jetzige) Erde' gegenüberstellen." (*Der Judasbrief / Der zweite Petrusbrief*, 1994, 227).

[410] Regarding the use of Ps 90:4 in Jewish traditions cf. R. Bauckham, *Jude, 2 Peter*, 1983, 306–310.

[411] Cf. W. Schrage, "'Ein Tag ist beim Herrn wie tausend Jahre, und tausend Jahre sind wie ein Tag'. 2 Petr 3,8", *Glaube und Eschatologie* (FS W.G. Kümmel), 1985, 267–275; H. Paulsen, *op. cit.*, 163–165.

parousia and the judgement never take place.[412] The author's assurance that the promise will be fulfilled even if the time is prolonged, is in agreement with the well-documented ancient Jewish way of thought, with an important point of reference in Hab 2:3 (cf. 1QpHab 7:5-12; LXX Sir 35:19).[413] The question is, however, what the main perspective is in this case. There is not much to be found in that connection in the negatively formulated argumentation in 2 Pet 3:9a. The following positive argument is more important. It is there that the central thoughts are expressed.

In v. 9b the conception of *God's long-suffering* is introduced. The delay of the parousia and the judgement are traced to that. Μακροθυμία in the LXX normally renders MT:s ארך אפים. In ancient Jewish literature God's long-suffering often functions as a factor which delays 'the wrath', manifested in an impending punishment (Wis 15:1; LXX Sir 35:19; 4 Ezra 7:74; *2 Bar.* 21:20-21; 59:6). That God is long-suffering means that he delays the act of judgement and that he gives some respite before the punishment is enacted.[414]

This aspect is now seen to be highly relevant regarding the *dor* of the Flood and other similar *dorot* and collectives in the early Jewish world of thought. As an example we can take *Mek.* Ex 15:6:

> "You gave an extension of time (ארכה) to the *dor* of the Flood, that they might repent (לעשׂות תשׁובה), but they did not repent... You gave an extension of time to the men of the Tower (i.e. the *dor* of Dispersion), that they might repent, but they did not repent... You gave an extension of time to the men of Sodom, that they might repent, bud they did not repent..."

It was closely related to the conception in question that God gave a respite before he carried out the punishment.[415] We can note that in the example given, among others, the *dor* of the Flood and the men of Sodom are referred to together - cf. 2 Pet 2:5-7! It is especially interesting with respect to the *dor* of the Flood to note that the 120

---

[412] Cf. BDR § 180,6: ..."hält sich nicht zaudernd zurück von der Erfüllung der Verheissung". Cf. J.H. Neyrey, "The Form and Background of the Polemic in 2 Peter", *JBL* 99, 1980, 414 f.

[413] See A. Strobel, *Untersuchungen zum eschatologischen Verzögerungsproblem*, 1961, 87-97, where the argumentation in vs. 8 f. is interpreted as building in essentials on the tradition from Hab 2:3.

[414] Cf. A. Strobel, *op. cit.,* 91; W. Harnisch, *Eschatologische Existenz*, 1973, 108. Neyrey demonstrates that in both Jewish and Greek sources we find it stated that divine punishment is delayed for purposes of repentance (*op. cit.*, 423-427). Regarding God's long-suffering in this situation see further e.g. *1 Enoch* 60:5; *Num. Rab.* 14:6 (60a).

[415] Cf. above p. 31 f.

years in Gen 6:3 are also seen from this perspective in the Targum: God gave the *dor* of the Flood such a long respite so that they would repent, but they did not (*Tg. Neof.* ad loc.; cf likewise *Tg. Onq.* ad loc.). Is it this interpretation of the Scriptures that is also mirrored in 1 Pet 3:20?[416] In any case we also find there - within the framework of the New Testament Petrine writings - the same view of God's behaviour before the Flood clearly expressed: "God's patience (μακροθυμία) waited in the days of Noah".

The purpose of the respite is made clear in the texts referred to. The intention was that people who had turned their backs on God in disobedience, would *repent*. That was certainly the aim of Noah's preaching (see above).

When it is mentioned, as an argument for the delay of the *parousia* in 2 Pet 3:9, that God is long-suffering (μακροθυμεῖ) as he does not wish anyone to be lost but that all shall reach repentance, this accordingly fits in totally with perspective of the Flood and the *dor* of the Flood.

It can thus be seen that the argumentation in 2 Pet 3 in no way contains a number of unconnected thoughts and motifs from the ancient Jewish world of ideas, which have been picked and coordinated *ad hoc* due to the current situation. There is a common element throughout. One can see a clear structure. After the reference to the Flood in v. 6 the author moves in a conceptual sphere which is related to the *dor* of the Flood. The second, eschatalogical end of the world is approaching, and that which happens before then has its *typos* in what happened to the *dor* before the first end, the catastrophy of the Flood.

This is important with respect to the perspective backwards in time. The idea of the people of the eschatalogical fulfilment as an evil *genea* with forerunners in faithless and sinful *dorot/geneai* in the history of the world and Israel, has been shown to have deep roots in synoptic tradition. In a number of cases the Synoptics associate to 'the *dor* of the Wilderness' (Mt 12:39; 16:4 et al.). But associations are also made to 'the *dor* of the Flood'. In two passages in the Synoptics the situation before and at the *parousia* is compared with the situation of דור המבול when the punishment fell (Mt 24:37 ff. and Lk 17:26 ff.).[417] We should note that the reference to the situation at the Flood is preceded in both cases by statements about ἡ γενεὰ αὕτη – completely different statements in the two Gospels but both about 'this *genea*'. As has been discussed in more detail above, this shows an association between 'this

---

[416] Cf. Bo Reicke, *The Disobedient Spirits*, 1946, 138.

[417] In Lk the reference to the *dor* of the Flood is combined with a reference to the men of Sodom - cf. 2 Pet. 2:5–7.

genea' and 'the *dor* of the Flood' in these cases.[418] The eschatological period before the end of the world (at the *parousia*) has arrived. It is therefore important to be constantly awake[419] and be prepared for the return of the Son of Man. Otherwise a catastrophe is waiting. In a similar way to the *dor* of the Flood, the *genea* that denies and rejects the Son of Man goes to its doom (Mt 12:41 f. et al.).

When the author of 2 Pet orients his counter-arguments against the dissidents from the typologically applied conception of the Flood and the *dor* of the Flood, he thus falls back on a tradition which is well documented in the Synoptics and there traced back to the teaching of Jesus[420] and uses it in the current situation.

As to the question of affinity between 2 Pet 3:3–13 and any special synoptic material regarding the presentation, a closer look shows that it is primarily the later part of the eschatological discourse in *Matthew* (Mt 24:34 ff.) that comes into focus. There are striking similarities between the description in 2 Pet and this passage.

1. 2 Pet uses the expression (Jesus') παρουσία (1:16; 3:4: cf. 3:12), a term which is not used in the Gospels with the exception of Mt 24, where, in contrast, it can be found several times (vs. 3, 27, 37, 39).

2. In the Mt passage there is to be found the *logion* about 'this *genea'*, which will not pass away until the end of the world and the *parousia*, at the same time as it is emphasized that no one knows the day and the hour (vs. 34-36)[421] – in 2 Pet there is the same eschatalogical direction in a *dor/genea* typological perspective while the uncertainty about the time for the eschatalogical end is a central point which is strongly stressed.

3. In the assurance as to the reliability of the statement it is said in the synoptic *logion*: "Heaven and earth will pass away (παρελεύσεται), but..." (v.35 par. Mk 13:31, Lk 21:33) – in 2 Pet it is said: Then (i.e. when the day of the Lord comes) "the heavens will pass away (παρελεύσονται)" (v. 10).

4. In Mt the 'this *genea*' statement (together with a marking of the uncertainty regarding the day and the hour) is followed by a Flood-typological exposition (vs. 37-42) – in 2 Pet there is a Flood-typological outlook.

5. In Mt the comparison with the Flood is followed by the parable of

---

418 Above chapters 8 and 6b respectively.

419 Regarding the menaing of the term 'wakefulness' in the Synoptics see E. Löve-stam, *Spiritual Wakefulness in the New Testament*, 1963, 78 ff.

420 Cf. 2 Pet 3:2b!

421 Par. Mk 13:30–32, Lk 21:32 f.

the thief at night (vs. 42-44)[422] – in 2 Pet it is said in this context: ..."the day of the Lord will come like a thief" (v. 10).

6. After the parable of the thief and its application Mt has the parable of the two servants, of whom one is found faithful by his master at his arrival, while the other is convinced that his master will not come so soon and "begins to beat his fellow servants, and eats and drinks with the drunken" but is surprised by the appearance of his lord and receives his punishment (vs. 45-51) – 2 Pet speaks against those who spread false doctrines, who scornfully deny the hope of Jesus' *parousia* and whose actions within the congregation are described in a way that brings to mind the unwise steward, although the description in the letter is more detailed and colourful.[423]

The affinity in the two passages is so substantial that it is difficult to avoid the conclusion that in both cases we find ourselves, in one way or another, in the same stream of tradition.[424] That then confirms what has been stated above concerning the perspective backwards as regards the argument with the dissidents in 2 Pet 3:3–13.

---

[422] As for the thief imagery in this case see E. Lövestam, *op. cit.*, 95–107.

[423] Cf. D. Wenham, "Being 'Found' on the Last Day: New Light on 2 Peter 3.10 and 2 Corinthians 5.3", *NTS* 33, 1987, 477; P. Dschulnigg, "Der theologische Ort des Zweiten Petrusbriefes", *BZ* 33, 1989, 170.

[424] As regards the relationship to Mt – cf. also P. Dschulnigg, *op. cit.*, 168–170 – it is worth noting that Mt contains more material on Peter than the other Gospels and that Peter is given a prominent place there; as U. Luz puts it: "Es ist...richtig, dass es eine gewisse Nähe zwischen Mt und dem 'petrinischen' Christentum gibt" (*Das Evangelium nach Matthäus* I, 1985, 74).

BIBLIOGRAPHY

Abbreviations

For abbreviations of biblical and other ancient texts, just as of journals, series etc., see: "Instructions for Contributors", *Journal of Biblical Literature* 107 (1988), 579–596.

Literature

Aalen, S., *Die Begriffe 'Licht' und 'Finsternis' im Alten Testament, im Spätjudentum und im Rabbinismus* (Skrifter utg. av Det Norske Vidensk.-Akad. i Oslo, II. Hist.-Filos.Kl. 1951:1), Oslo 1951.

Achtemeier, P. J., "Miracles and the Historical Jesus: A Study of Mark 9:14–29", *CBQ* 37, 1975, 471–491.

Aichinger, H., "Zur Traditionsgeschichte der Epileptiker-Perikope Mk 9,14–29 par Mt 17,14–21 par Lk 9,37–43a" in A. Fuchs (ed.), *Studien zum NT und seiner Umwelt* Ser. A, Bd 3, Wien–München 1978, 114–143.

Albright, W. F., "Some Remarks on the Song of Moses in Deuteronomy XXXII", *VT* 9, 1959, 339–346.

Allmen, D. von, "L´apocalyptique juive et le retard de la parousie en II Pierre 3:1–13", *RTP* 16, 1966, 255–274.

Attridge, Harold W., *The Epistle to the Hebrews*. Ed. by H. Koester. Philadelphia 1989.

Aune, David E., *Prophecy in Early Christianity and the Ancient Mediterranean World*, Grand Rapids 1983.

Bacher, W., *Die Agada der Tannaiten*. I: 2. Aufl. Strassburg 1903. II: Strassburg 1890.

Baker, David L., "Typology and the Christian Use of the Old Testament", *SJT* 29, 1976, 137–157.

Balz, H. - Wanke, G., φοβέω κτλ., *TWNT* 9, 1973, 186–216.

Bernett, P. W., "The Jewish Sign Prophets – A.D. 40–70. Their Intentions and Origin", *NTS* 27, 1981, 679–697.

Basser, Herbert W., *Midrashic Interpretations of the Song of Moses* (Am. Univ. Studies VII:2), New York –Frankfort on the Main–Berne 1984.

Bauckham, Richard J., *Jude, 2 Peter* (WBC), Waco, Texas 1983.

—, "2 Peter: An Account of Research", *ANRW* II, 25:5, 1988, 3713–3752.

Bauer, Walter, *Griechisch-deutsches Wörterbuch zu den Schriften des Neuen Testaments und der frühchristlichen Literatur*. 6., völlig neu bearbeitete Aufl. hrsg. von K.u.B. Aland. Berlin-New York 1988.

Bauernfeind, Otto, *Kommentar und Studien zur Apostelgeschichte*. Mit einer Einleitung von M. Hengel. Hrsg. von V. Metelmann (WUNT 22). Tübingen 1980.

Beasley-Murray, George R., *A Commentary on Mark Thirteen*, London 1957.

—, *Jesus and the Last Days. The Interpretation of the Olivet Discourse*.Peabody, Mass., 1993.

Berger, Klaus, "Streit um Gottes Vorsehung. Zur Position der Gegner im 2. Petrusbrief", *Tradition and Re-interpretation in Jewish and Early Christian Literature* (FS C. H. Lebram), Leiden 1986, 121–135.

Beyer, Klaus, *Semitische Syntax im Neuen Testament* (SUNT 1), Bd I:1. Göttingen 1962.

Black, Matthew, *An Aramaic Approach to the Gospels and Acts.* 3rd ed. With an Appendix on 'The Son of Man' by G. Vermes. Oxford 1967.

Blank, Sheldon H., "The Death of Zechariah in Rabbinic Literature", *HUCA* XII–XIII, 1937–38, 327–346.

Blass, F.-Debrunner, A.-Rehkopf, F., *Grammatik des neutestamentlichen Griechisch.* 14., völlig neubearbeitete und erweiterte Aufl., Göttingen 1976.

Böcher, Otto, *Das Neue Testament und die dämonischen Mächte* (SBS 58), Stuttgart 1972.

Bonnard, Pierre, *L'Evangile selon Saint Matthieu* (CNT), Neuchatel 1963.

Bornkamm, G.-Barth, G.-Held, H.J., *Überlieferung und Auslegung im Matthäus evangelium* (WMANT 1), 4., vermehrte Aufl., Neukirchen 1965.

Botterweck, G. J.–Freedman, D. N.–Lundbom, J., דוֹר *dôr, TWAT* II, 1977, 181–195.

Bowman, John, *The Gospel of Mark. The New Christian Jewish Passover Haggadah* (SPB 8), Leiden 1965.

Bovon, François, *Das Evangelium nach Lukas* I (EKKNT), Zürich-Neukirchen/Vluyn 1989.

Brandenburger, Egon, *Markus 13 und die Apokalyptik* (FRLANT 134), Göttingen 1984.

Braun, Herbert, *An die Hebräer* (HNT 14), Tübingen 1984.

—, *Qumran und das Neue Testament* I–II, Tübingen 1966.

Bruce, F. F., *Commentary on the Book of the Acts. The Englich Text with Introduction, Exposition and Notes*, London 1954 (1972).

Buchanan, G. W., *To the Hebrews. Translation, Comment and Conclusions* (AB), Garden city, New York 1972.

Büchsel, Friedrich, γενεά κτλ., *TWNT* 1, 1933, 660–663.

Bultmann, Rudolf, *Die Geschichte der synoptischen Tradition* (FRLANT NF 12), 7. Aufl., Göttingen 1967.

Burch, Vacher, "The Petitioning Blood of the Prophets (Luke XI, 49–51)", *ExpTim* 30, 1918-19, 329–330.

Charles, J. Daryl, "Jude's Use of Pseudepigraphical Source-Material as Part of a Literary Strategy", *NTS* 37, 1991, 130–145.

Charlesworth, James H., *Jesus within Judaism. New Light from Exciting Archaeological Discoveries,* London 1989.

Christoffersson, Olle, *The Earnest Expectation of the Creature. The Flood-Tradition as Matrix of Romans 8:18–27* (ConBNT 23), Stockholm 1990.

Collins, J. J., "Sibylline Oracles", *OTP* I, 1983, 317–472.

Conzelmann, Hans, *Die Mitte der Zeit. Studien zur Theologie des Lukas* (BHT 17), 5. Aufl., Tübingen 1964.

Coppens, J., "Les logia du Fils de l' homme dans l'évangile de Marc", *L'Evangile selon Marc. Tradition et rédaction* (BETL 34), nouv. éd. 1988, 487–528.

Cotter, Wendy J., "The Parable of the Children in the Market-place, Q (Lk) 7:31–35:

An Examination of the Parable´s Image and Significance", *NovT* 29, 1987, 289–304.

Cranfield, C. E. B., *The Gospel according to Saint Mark* (CGTC), Cambridge 1959.

Cullmann, Oscar, *Die Christologie des Neuen Testaments.* 2. Aufl. Tübingen 1958.

—, *Heil als Geschichte. Heilsgeschichtliche Existenz im Neuen Testament*, Tübingen 1965.

Dalman, Gustaf, *Die Worte Jesu. Mit Berücksichtigung des nachkanonischen jüdischen Schrifttums und der aramäischen Sprache.* Bd I: Einleitung und wichtige Begriffe. 2. Aufl. Leipzig 1930.

—, *Jesus–Jeschua. Die drei Sprachen Jesu. Jesus in der Synagoge, auf dem Berge, beim Passahmahl, am Kreuz.*Leipzig 1922.

Daniélou, Jean, "Eschatologie sadocite et eschatologie chrétienne", *Les manuscrits de la Mer Morte*, Paris: Presses universitaires de France 1957, 111–125.

—, *Sacramentum futuri. Etudes sur les origines de la typologie biblique*, Paris 1950.

Daube, D., "'For they know not what they do': Luke 23,34", *Studia Patristica* IV (TU 79), Berlin 1961, 58–70.

Davies, W. D., *Paul and Rabbinic Judaism. Some Rabbinic Elements in Pauline Theology*, London 1965.

Davies, W. D. - Allison, D. C., *A Critical and Exegetical Commentary on the Gospel according to Saint Matthew* (ICC) I-II, Edinburgn 1988-1991.

Derrett, J. Duncan M., "'You build the Tombs of the Prophets' (Lk. 11,47–51, Mt 23,29–31)", *Studia Evangelica* IV (TU 102), Berlin 1968, 187–193.

Dexinger, F., *Sturz der Göttersöhne oder Engel vor der Sintflut? Versuch sines Neuverständnisses von Genesis 6,2–4 unter Berücksichtigung der religionsge schichtlichen Methode* (Wiener Beiträge zur Theologie 13), Wien 1966.

Dodd, C. H., *The Parables of the Kingdom.* Rev. ed. London 1961.

Drazin, Israel, *Targum Onkelos to Deuteronomy. An English Translation of the Text. With Analysis and Commentary.* New York 1982.

Dschulnigg, Peter., "Der theologische Ort des Zweiten Petrusbriefes", *BZ* 33, 1989, 161–177.

Duling, D. C., "Testament of Solomon", *OTP* I, 1983, 935–987.

Dupont, Jacques, *Les trois apocalypses synoptiques. Marc 13; Matthieu 24-25; Luc 21* (LD 121), Paris 1985.

Edwards, Richard A., *The Sign of Jonah in the Theology of the Evangelists and Q* (SBT II:18), London 1971.

Ellis, E. Earle, *The Gospel of Luke* (NCB), Grand Rapids-London 1974 (1983).

—, *The Old Testament in Early Christianity. Canon and Interpretation in the Light of Modern Research* (WUNT 54), Tübingen 1991.

Evans, C. F., *Saint Luke* (TPI NTComm), London-Philadelphia 1990.

Feuillet, A., "Le discours de Jésus sur la ruine du temple d´après Marc XIII et Luc XXI, 5–36", *RB* 55, 1948, 481–502 and *RB* 56, 1949, 61–92.

Filson, Floyd V., *A Commentary on the Gospel according to St. Matthew* (Black´s NT Comm), London 1960.

Fitzmyer, Joseph A., *The Gospel According to Luke. Introduction, Translation and Notes* (AB). I-II. New York 1982-1985.

Fornberg, Tord, *An Early Church in a Pluralistic Society. A Study of 2 Peter* (ConBNT 9). Lund 1977.

Frankemölle, Hubert, *Jahwebund und Kirche Christi. Studien zur Form- und Traditionsgeschichte des 'Evangeliums' nach Matthäus* (NTAbh NF 10). Münster in Westf. 1974.

Freedman, D. N.–Lundbom, J., see Botterweck, G.

Friedrich, Gerhard, προφήτης κτλ.: "D. Propheten und Prophezeien im Neuen Testament", *TWNT* 6, 1959, 829–863.

Fuchs, E. - Reymond, P., *La deuxième épitre de Saint Pierre. L´épitre de Saint Jude* (CNT), Paris 1980.

Garland, David E., *The Intention of Matthew 23* (NovTSup 52), Leiden 1979.

Gärtner, Bertil, "The Habakkuk Commentary (DSH) and the Gospel of Matthew", *ST* 8, 1954, 1–24.

Geiger, Ruthild, *Die Lukanischen Endzeitreden. Studien zur Eschatologie des Lukas-Evangeliums* (Europäische Hochschulschriften XXIII:16), Bern-Frankfurt a.M. 1973.

Gerhardsson, Birger, *The Testing of God´s Son (Matt 4:1–11 & par). An Analysis of an Early Christian Midrash* (ConBNT 2:1), Lund 1966.

Gerleman, Gillis, "דּוֹר *dôr* Generation", *Theol. Handwörterbuch zum AT* I, 1971, 443–445.

Ginzberg, L., *The Legends of the Jews* I-VI. Philadelphia 1925-1938.

Giversen, Søren, *Thomasevangeliet. Indledning, oversættelse og kommentarer.* København 1959.

Glombitza, Otto, "Das Zeichen des Jona. (Zum Verständnis von Matth. XII.38–42)", *NTS* 8, 1962, 359–366.

Gnilka, Joachim, *Das Evangelium nach Markus* (EKKNT) I-II, Zürich-Neukirchen/ Vluyn 1978-79.

—, *Das Matthäusevangelium* (HTKNT) I-II, Freiburg-Basel-Wien 1986-88.

—, *Der Philipperbrief* (HTKNT), Freiburg-Basel-Wien 1968.

Goppelt, L., *Typos. Die typologische Deutung des Alten Testaments im Neuen* (BFCT II:43), Gütersloh 1939.

Grässer, Erich, *An die Hebräer* (EKKNT) I, Zürich-Einsiedeln-Köln-Neukirchen 1990.

Grossfeld, Bernard, *The Targum Onqelos to Deuteronomy. Translated, with Apparatus and Notes* (The Aramaic Bible 9). Wilmington 1988.

Grundmann, Walter, *Das Evangelium nach Lukas* (THKNT), Berlin 1961.

—, *Das Evangelium nach Matthäus* (THKNT), Berlin 1968.

Guillet, Jacques, "Cette génération infidèle et dévoyée", *RSR* 35, 1948, 275–281.

Gundry, Robert H., *Matthew. A Commentary on His Literary and Theological Art*, Grand Rapids 1982.

Haenchen, Ernst, *Der Weg Jesu. Eine Erklärung des Markus-Evangeliums und der kanonischen Parallelen*, Berlin 1966.

—, *Die Apostelgeschichte* (MeyerK), 7. Aufl., Göttingen 1977.

Hagner, Donald A., *Hebrews* (Good News Comm.), San Francisco, 1983.

—, *The Use of the Old and New Testaments in Clement of Rome* (NovT Suppl. 34), Leiden 1973.

Hahn, Ferdinand, *Christologische Hoheitstitel. Ihre Geschichte im frühen Christentum.* 2. Aufl. Göttingen 1964.

—, "Die Rede von der Parusie des Menschensohnes Markus 13", *Jesus und der Menschensohn* (FS Anton Vögtle), Freiburg-Basel-Wien 1975, 240–266.

Hare, Douglas R. A., *The Theme of Jewish Persecution of Christians in the Gospel according to St. Matthew* (SNTSMS 6), Cambridge 1967.

Harnisch, Wolfgang, *Eschatologische Existenz. Ein exegetischer Beitrag zum Sachanliegen von 1. Thessalonicher 4,13–5,11* (FRLANT 110), Göttingen 1973.

Hartman, Lars, "An early Example of Jewish Exegesis: 1 Enoch 10:16–11:2", *Neot* 17, 1983, 16–27.

—, *Prophecy Interpreted. The Formation of some Jewish Apocalyptic Texts and of the Eschatological Discourse Mark 13 par.* (ConBNT 1), Lund 1966.

—, "Reading Luke 17, 20–37", *The Four Gospels 1992* (FS Frans Neirynck) (BETL 100). Vol. 2, Leuven 1992, 1663–1675.

Hasler, V., "γενεά Generation, Geschlecht", *EWNT* I, 1980, 579–581.

Hawthorne, Gerald F., *Philippians* (WBC), Waco 1983.

Held, H. J., see Bornkamm, G.

Hermaniuk, Maxime, *La Parabole Evangélique* (Universitas Catholica Lovaniensis, Ser. II, Vol. 38), Louvain-Paris 1947.

Hoffmann, Paul, *Studien zur Theologie der Logienquelle* (NTAbh NF 8), Münster in Westf. 1972.

Hofius, Otfried, *Katapausis. Die Vorstellung vom endzeitlichen Ruheort im Hebräerbrief* (WUNT 11), Tübingen 1970.

Holtz, Traugott, *Jesus aus Nazareth*, Berlin 1979.

Hooker, Morna D., "The Son of Man and the Synoptic Problem", *The Four Gospels 1992* (FS F. Neirynck) (BETL 100). Vol. 1, Leuven 1992, 189–201.

Jeremias, Joachim, *Die Gleichnisse Jesu.* 4., neu bearbeitete Aufl. Göttingen 1956.

—, *Die Sprache des Lukasevangeliums. Redaktion und Tradition im Nicht-Markusstoff des dritten Evangeliums* (MeyerK Sonderband), Göttingen 1980.

—, *Heiligengräber in Jesu Umwelt (Mt. 23,29; Lk. 11,47). Eine Untersuchung zur Volksreligion der Zeit Jesu*, Göttingen 1958.

—, *Jesus´ Promise to the Nations* (SBT 24), red. ed. London 1967.

—, 'Ιωνᾶς, *TWNT* 3, 1938, 410–413.

—, Μωυσῆς, *TWNT* 4, 1942, 852–878.

—, *Neutestamentliche Theologie. I.Teil: Die Verkündigung Jesu*, Gütersloh 1971.

Johnsson, William G., "The Pilgrimage Motif in the Book of Hebrews", *JBL* 97, 1978, 239–251.

Kahmann, Johannes, "The Second Letter of Peter and the Letter of Jude. Their Mutual Relationship", *The New Testament in Early Christianity* (BETL 86), Leuven 1989, 105–121.

Kaplan, C., "The Flood in the Book of Enoch and Rabbinics", *Journal of the Society of Oriental Research* 15, 1931, 22–24.

Käsemann, Ernst, "Eine Apologie der urchristlichen Eschatologie", *ZTK* 49, 1952, 272–296.

—, *Essays on New Testament Themes* (SBT 41), London 1964.

Kasper, Walter, *Jesus der Christus. Grundriss und Aufsätze zur Christologie*, Leipzig 1981.

Kertelge, Karl, *Die Wunder Jesu im Markusevangelium. Eine redaktionsgeschichtliche Untersuchung* (SANT 23), München 1970.

Knoch, Otto, *Eigenart und Bedeutung der Eschatologie im theologischen Aufriss des ersten Clemensbriefes. Eine auslegungsgeschichtliche Untersuchung* (Theophaneia

17), Bonn 1964.

Kuhn, Karl Georg, *Der tannaitische Midrasch Sifre zu Numeri* (Rabbinische Texte hrsg. v. G. Kittel u. K. H. Rengstorf, 2. Reihe, 3. Bd.), Stuttgart 1959.

—, "Die in Palästina gefundenen hebräischen Texte und das Neue Testament", *ZTK* 47, 1950, 192–211.

Kümmel, Werner Georg, "Das Verhalten Jesus gegenüber und das Verhalten des Menschensohns. Markus 8,38 par und Lukas 12,3f par Matthäus 10,32f", R. Pesch-R. Schnackenburg (ed.), *Jesus und der Menschensohn* (FS A. Vögtle), Freiburg-Basel-Wien 1975, 210–224.

—, *Die Theologie des Neuen Testaments* (Grundrisse zum Neuen Testament 3), Göttingen 1969.

—, *Einleitung in das Neue Testament*. 21., erneut ergänzte Aufl. Heidelberg 1983.

—, "Jesusforschung seit 1981. V. Der persönliche Anspruch sowie der Prozess und Kreuzestod Jesu", *TRu* 56, 1991, 391–420.

—, *Promise and Fulfilment. The Eschatological Message of Jesus* (SBT 23), London 1957.

Künzi, Martin, *Das Naherwartungslogion Markus 9,1 par. Geschichte seiner Auslegung mit einem Nachwort zur Auslegungsgeschichte von Markus 13,30 par.* (BGBE 21), Tübingen 1977.

Lagrange, M.-J., *Evangile selon Saint Luc* (Ebib), 8. éd., Paris 1948.

—, *Evangile selon Saint Marc* (Ebib), éd. corrigée et augmentée, Paris 1947.

Lambrecht, J., *Die Redaktion der Markus-Apokalypse: Literarische Analyse und Strukturuntersuchung* (AnBib 28), Rom 1967.

Lane, William L., *Hebrews 1–8* (WBC), Dallas 1991.

Leaney, A. R. C., *A Commentary on the Gospel according to St. Luke* (Black's NT Comm.), 2nd ed., London 1966.

Légasse, Simon, "L'oracle contre 'cette génération' (Mt 23,34–36 par. Lc 11,49–51) et la polémique judéo-chrétienne dans la source du logia", *Logia. Les paroles de Jésus – the sayings of Jesus* (Mémorial J. Coppens) (BETL 59), Leuven 1982, 237–256.

Leivestad, R., *Hvem ville Jesus være?* Oslo 1982.

Lewis, Jack P., *A Study of the Interpretation of Noah and the Flood in Jewish and Christian Literature,* Leiden 1968.

Linton, Olof, "The Demand for a Sign from Heaven (Mk 8,11–12 and Parallels)", *ST* 19, 1965, 112–129.

—, "The Parable of the Children's Game. Baptist and Son of Man (Matt. XI. 16–19 = Luke VII. 31–35: A Synoptic Text-Critical, Structural and Exegetical Investigation", *NTS* 22, 1976, 159–179.

Ljungman, Henrik, *Das Gesetz erfüllen. Matth. 5,17ff. und 3,15 untersucht* (LUÅ NF I, 50:6), Lund 1954.

Loader, J. A., *A Tale of Two Cities. Sodom and Gomorrah in the Old Testament, early Jewish and early Christian Traditions* (Contributions to Biblical Exegesis and Theology 1), Kampen 1990.

Lohmeyer, Ernst, *Das Evangelium des Markus* (MeyerK), Göttingen 1951.

—, *Der Brief an die Philipper* (MeyerK), Göttingen 1953.

Lüdemann, Gerd, *Das frühe Christentum nach den Traditionen der Apostelgeschichte. Ein Kommentar,* Göttingen 1987.

Lührmann, Dieter, *Die Redaktion der Logienquelle. Anhang: Zur weiteren Überlief-*

erung der Logienquelle (WMANT 33), Neukirchen-Vluyn 1969.

Luz, Ulrich, *Das Evangelium nach Matthäus* I-II (EKKNT), Zürich-Einsiedeln-Köln–Neukirchen 1985-1990.

Lövestam, Evald, *Apostlagärningarna*, Stockholm 1988.

—, "Der Rettungsappell in Ag 2,40", *ASTI* 12, 1983, 84–92.

—, "Eschatologie und Tradition im 2. Petrusbrief", *The New Testament Age* (FS Bo Reicke), I-II, Macon 1984, 287–300.

—, "Jésus Fils de David chez les Synoptiques", *ST* 28, 1974, 97–109.

—, *Son and Saviour. A Study of Acts 13,32–37. With an Appendix: 'Son of God' in the Synoptic Gospels* (ConNT 18), Lund-Copenhagen 1961.

—, *Spiritual Wakefulness in the New Testament* (LUÅ NF I,55:3), Lund 1963.

—, *Spiritus blasphemia. Eine Studie zu Mk 3,28f par Mt 12,31f, Lk 12,10* (Scripta minora Regiae Societatis Humaniorum Litterarum Lundensis 1966-1967:1), Lund 1968.

—, "The ἡ γενεὰ αὕτη Eschatology in Mk 13,30 parr.", *L'Apocalypse johannique et l'Apocalyptique dans le Nouveau Testament* (BETL 53), Leuven 1980, 403–413.

—, "Urkyrkans skriftförståelse" in E. Lövestam, *Axplock. Nytestamentliga studier* (Religio 26), Lund 1987, 17–25.

Maddox, Robert, *The Purpose of Luke-Acts*, Göttingen 1982.

Manson, T. W., *The Sayings of Jesus as Recorded in the Gospels according to St. Matthew and St. Luke . Arranged with Introduction and Commentary*, London 1971.

Marshall, Christopher D., *Faith as a Theme in Mark´s Narrative,* Cambridge 1989.

Marshall, I. Howard, *The Acts of the Apostles. An Introduction and Commentary* (Tyndale NT Comm.), Grand Rapids 1980.

—, *The Gospel of Luke. A Commentary on the Greek Text* (NIGTC), Exeter 1978.

Martin, Ralph P., *Philippians* (NCB), Grand Rapids-London 1980.

Mauser, Ulrich W., *Christ in the Wilderness. The Wilderness Theme in the Second Gospel and its Basis in the Biblical Tradition* (SBT 39), London 1963.

Mayer, Rudolf, *Die biblische Vorstellung vom Weltbrand. Eine Untersuchung über die Beziehungen zwischen Parsismus und Judentum* (Bonner Orientalische Studien, NSer 4), Bonn 1956.

Mayes, A. D. H., *Deuteronomy* (NCB), Grand Rapids-London 1979 (1987).

McArthur (ed.), *In Search of the Historical Jesus*, New York 1969.

McCasland, S. V., "Signs and Wonders", *JBL* 76, 1957, 149–152.

McCullough, J. C., "The Old Testament Quotations in Hebrews", *NTS* 26, 1980, 363–379.

McNamara, Martin, *The New Testament and the Palestinian Targum to the Pentateuch* (AnBib 27), Rom 1966.

Meier, Sam, "2 Peter 3:3–7 – An Early Jewish and Christian Response to Eschatological Skepticism", *BZ* 32, 1988, 255–257.

Meinertz, Max, "'Dieses Geschlecht' im Neuen Testament", *BZ* NF 1, 1957, 283–289.

Merk, Otto, "Das Reich Gottes in den lukanischen Schriften", *Jesus und Paulus* (FS W. G. Kümmel), Göttingen 1978, 201–220.

Metzger, B. M., "The Fourth Book of Ezra. With the Four Additional Chapters. A

New Translation and Introduction", *OTP* I, 1983, 517–559.

Michaelis, Wilhelm, *Der Herr verzieht nicht die Verheissung*, Bern 1942.

—, πάσχω κτλ., *TWNT* 5, 1954, 903–939.

Miller, Robert J., "The Rejection of the Prophets in Q", *JBL* 107, 1988, 225–240.

M'Neile, Alan Hugh, *The Gospel according to St. Matthew. The Greek Text with Introduction, Notes, and Indices*, London-Melbourne-Toronto-New York 1915 (1965).

Moule, C. F. D., "Fulfilment-Words in the New Testament: Use and Abuse", *NTS* 14, 1968, 293–320.

Mussner, Franz, "Der nicht erkannte Kairos (Mt 11,16–19 = Lk 7,31–35)", *Bib* 40, 1959, 599–612.

—, "Wege zum Selbstbewusstsein Jesu", *BZ* NF 12, 1968, 161–172.

—, "Wer ist 'dieses Geschlecht' in Mk 13,30 parr.?", *Kairos* NF 29, 1987, 23–28.

Müller, Mogens, *Der Ausdruck 'Menschensohn' in den Evangelien. Voraussetzungen und Bedeutung* (ATDan 17), Leiden 1984.

Neyrey, Jerome H., "The Form and Background of the Polemic in 2 Peter", *JBL* 99, 1980, 407–431.

Nixon, R. E., *The Exodus in the New Testament*, London 1963.

Noack, Bent, *Satanás und Soteria. Untersuchungen zur neotestamentlichen Dämonologie,* København 1948.

Nolan, Brian M., "Some Observations on the Parousia and New Testament Eschatology", *ITQ* 36, 1969, 283–314.

Nolland, John, *Luke* I (WBC), Dallas 1989.

Oberlinner, L., "Die Stellung der 'Terminworte' in der eschatologischen Verkündigung des Neuen Testaments", *Gegenwart und Kommendes Reich* (FS Anton Vögtle), Stuttgart 1975, 51–66.

Paulsen, Henning, *Der zweite Petrusbrief und der Judasbrief* (MeyerK), Göttingen 1992.

Pearson, B. A., "1 Thessalonians 2:13–16: A Deutero-Pauline Interpretation", *HTR* 64, 1971, 79–94.

Percy, Ernst, *Die Botschaft Jesu. Eine traditionskritische und exegetische Untersuchung* (LUÅ NF I, 49:5), Lund 1953.

Perrin, N., *Rediscovering the Teaching of Jesus*, New York 1967.

Pesch, Rudolf, *Das Markusevangelium* I-II (HTKNT), Freiburg-Basel-Wien 1976-1977.

—, *Die Apostelgeschichte* I-II (EKKNT), Zürich-Einsiedeln-Köln-Neukirchen 1986.

—, *Naherwartungen. Tradition und Redaktion in Mk 13*, Düsseldorf 1968.

—, "Über die Autorität Jesu. Eine Rückfrage anhand des Bekenner- und Verleugnerspruchs Lk 12,8f par.", *Die Kirche des Anfangs* (FS H. Schürmann) (ETS 38), Leipzig 1977, 25–55.

Petzke, G., "Die historische Frage nach den Wundertaten Jesu. Dargestellt am Beispiel des Exorzismus Mark. IX.14–29 par", *NTS* 22, 1976, 180–204.

Polag, Athanasius, *Die Christologie der Logienquelle* (WMANT 45), Neukirchen-Vluyn 1977.

Prat, Ferdinand, "Cette génération", *RSR* 17, 1927, 316–324.

Rappaport, Salomo, "Der gerechte Lot. Bemerkung zu II Ptr 2,7.8", *ZNW* 29, 1930, 299–304.

Reicke, Bo, *The Disobedient Spirits and Christian Baptism. A Study of 1 Pet. III.19 and its Context* (ASNU 13), København 1946.

Reiser, Marius, *Die Gerichtspredigt Jesu. Eine Untersuchung zur eschatologischen Verkündigung Jesu und ihrem frühjüdischen Hintergrund* (NTAbh NF 23), Münster 1990.

Rengstorf, K. H., ἁμαρτωλός κτλ., *TWNT* 1, 1933, 320–337.

—, *Das Evangelium nach Lukas* (NTD). 9. durchgesehene und ergänzte Aufl., Göttingen 1962.

—, γογγύζω κτλ., *TWNT* 1, 1933, 727–737.

—, σημεῖον κτλ., *TWNT* 7, 1964, 199–268.

Riesenfeld, Harald, "De fientliga andarna. (Mk 9:14–29)", *SEÅ* 22-23, 1958, 64–74.

—, *Jésus transfiguré. L'arrière-plan du récit évangélique de la transfiguration de Notre-Seigneur* (ASNU 16), København 1947.

Roloff, Jürgen, "Anfänge der soteriologischen Deutung des Todes Jesu (Mk. X.45 und Lk. XXII.27)", *NTS* 19, 1972, 38–64.

—, *Die Apostelgeschichte* (NTD), Göttingen 1981.

Rosenbaum, M.-Silbermann, A.M., *Pentateuch with Targum Onkelos, Haphtaroth and Prayers for Sabbath and Rashi´s Commentary. Translated into English and Annotated.* I-II. London 1946.

Rothkoff, A.–Aberbach, M., "Golden calf", *EncJud* 7, 1971, 709–713.

Rubinkiewicz, Ryszard, *Die Eschatologie von Henoch 9–11 und das Neue Testament* (ÖBS 6), Klosterneuburg 1984.

Rudolph, W., *Joel–Amos–Obadja–Jona* (KAT), Gütersloh 1971.

Schelkle, Karl Hermann, *Die Petrusbriefe. Der Judasbrief* (HTKNT), Freiburg-Basel-Wien 1961.

Schenk, Wolfgang, *Die Philipperbriefe des Paulus. Kommentar*, Stuttgart-Berlin-Köln-Mainz 1984.

—, "Tradition und Redaktion in der Epileptiker-Perikope Mk 9,14–29", *ZNW* 63, 1972, 76–94.

Schiffman, Lawrence H., *The Eschatological Community of the Dead Sea Scrolls. A Study of the Rule of the Congregation* (SBLMS 38), Atlanta 1989.

Schlier, Heinrich, *Mächte und Gewalten im Neuen Testament* (QD 3), Freiburg i.B. 1958.

Schlosser, J., "Les jours de Noé et de Lot. A propos de *Luc*, XVII,26–30", *RB* 80, 1973, 13–36.

Schmidt, D., "1 Thess 2:13–16: Linguistic Evidence for an Interpolation", *JBL* 102, 1983, 269–279.

Schmitt, G., "Das Zeichen des Jona", *ZNW* 69, 1978, 123–129.

Schnackenburg, Rudolf, "Der eschatologische Abschnitt Lk 17,20–37", *Mélanges bibliques* (FS B. Rigaux), Gembloux 1970, 213–234.

—, *Gottes Herrschaft und Reich. Eine biblisch-theologische Studie.* 2., durchge sehene und ergänzte Aufl., Freiburg-Basel-Wien 1961.

—, *Matthäusevangelium* I (Die Neue Echter Bibel), Würzburg 1985.

Schneider, Gerhard, *Die Apostelgeschichte* I-II (HTKNT), Freiburg-Basel-Wien 1980-1982.

Schneider, Johannes, ἔρχομαι κτλ., *TWNT* 2, 1935, 662–682.

Schniewind, Julius, *Das Evangelium nach Markus* (NTD), 8. Auflage, Göttingen

1958.

—, *Das Evangelium nach Matthäus* (NTD), 7. Auflage, Göttingen 1954.

Schrage, Wolfgang, "'Ein Tag ist beim Herrn wie tausend Jahre, und tausend Jahre sind wie ein Tag'. 2 Petr 3,8", *Glaube und Eschatologie* (FS W. G. Kümmel), Tübingen 1985, 267–275.

Schrenk, Gottlob, διαλέγομαι κτλ., *TWNT* 2, 1935, 93–98.

Schulz, Siegfried, *Die Mitte der Schrift. Der Frühkatholizismus im Neuen Testament als Herausforderung an den Protestantismus*, Stuttgart-Berlin 1976.

—, *Q. Die Spruchquelle der Evangelisten*, Zürich 1972.

Schweizer, Eduard, *Das Evangelium nach Markus* (NTD), Göttingen 1967.

—, *Das Evangelium nach Matthäus* (NTD), Göttingen 1973.

Schüpphaus, Joachim, *Die Psalmen Salomos. Ein Zeugnis Jerusalemer Theologie und Frömmigkeit in der Mitte des vorchristlichen Jahrhunderts* (ALGHJ 7), Leiden 1977.

Schürer, Emil, *The History of the Jewish People in the Age of Jesus Christ (175 B.C.–A.D. 135)*. A New English Version revised and edited by G. Vermes, F. Millar, M. Black, M. Goodman. I-III:2. Edinburgh 1973–1987.

Schürmann, Heinz, *Das Lukasevangelium* I-II:1 (HTKNT), Freiburg-Basel-Wien 1969-1994.

—, "Die Redekomposition wider 'dieses Geschlecht' und seine Führung in der Redenquelle (vgl. Mt 23,1–39 par Lk 11,37–54). Bestand – Akoluthie – Kompositionsformen", *Studien zum Neuen Testament und seiner Umwelt* Ser. A, Bd 11, Linz 1986, 33–81.

Seesemann, H., πεῖρα κτλ., *TWNT* 6, 1959, 23–37.

Seidelin, P., "Das Jonaszeichen", *ST* 5, 1951, 119–131.

Sjöberg, Erik, *Der Menschensohn im äthiopischen Henochbuch* (Acta Reg. Societatis Humaniorum Litterarum Lundensis 41), Lund 1946.

—, *Gott und die Sünder im palästinischen Judentum nach dem Zeugnis der Tannaiten und der apokryphisch-pseudepigraphischen Literatur* (BWANT 4.F., H.27), Stuttgart 1939.

Soards, Marion L., "1 Peter, 2 Peter, and Jude as Evidence for a Petrine School", *ANRW* II,25:5, 1988, 3827–3849.

Stählin, Gustav, *Die Apostelgeschichte* (NTD), Göttingen 1962.

Steck, O.H., *Israel und das gewaltsame Geschick der Propheten. Untersuchungen zur Überlieferung des deuteronomistischen Geschichtsbildes im Alten Testament, Spätjudentum und Urchristentum* (WMANT 23), Neukirchen-Vluyn 1967.

Steinhauser, M.G., "Noah in his Generation: An Allusion in Luke 16,8b, 'εἰς τὴν γενεὰν τὴν ἑαυτῶν'", *ZNW* 79, 1988, 152–157.

Stendahl, Krister, "Matthew", *PCB*, 1962, 769–798.

Sterling, Gregory E., "Jesus as Exorcist: An Analysis of Matthew 17:14–20; Mark 9:14–29; Luke 9:37–43a", *CBQ* 55, 1993, 467–493.

Stern, David, "Jesus' Parables from the Perspective of Rabbinic Literature: The Example of the Wicked Husbandmen", in: Cl. Thoma–M. Wyschogrod (ed.), *Parable and Story in Judaism and Christianity*, New York 1989, 42–80.

Stolz, Fritz, "Zeichen und Wunder. Die prophetische Legitimation und ihre Geschichte", *ZTK* 69, 1972, 125–144.

Strack. H. L.–Billerbeck. P.(–Jeremias, J.–Adolph, K.), *Kommentar zum Neuen*

Testament aus Talmud und Misrasch, 1–4 (6), München 1922–1928 (1961).

Streeter, B. H., *The Four Gospels. A Study of Origins, Treating of the Manuscript Tradition, Sources, Authorship & Dates*, London 1924.

Strobel, August, *Untersuchungen zum eschatolgischen Verzögerungsproblem. Auf Grund der spätjüdisch-urchristlichen Geschichte von Habakuk 2,2 ff.* (NovTSup 2), Leiden-Köln 1961.

Swetnam, J., "Some Signs of Jonah", *Bib* 68, 1987, 74–79.

Tabachovitz, D., *Die Septuaginta und das Neue Testament. Stilstudien* (Acta Instituti Atheniensis Regni Sueciae, Ser in 8o, 4), Lund 1956.

Talbert, Charles H., "II Peter and the Delay of the Parousia", *VC* 20, 1966, 137–145.

Talmon, Shemaryahu, "The 'Desert Motif' in the Bible and in Qumran Literature", *Biblical Motifs. Origins and Transformations* (ed. A. Altmann), Cambridge, Mass., 1966, 31–63.

Taylor, Vincent, *The Gospel according to St. Mark. The Greek Text with Introduction, Notes, and Indexes*, London - New York 1957.

Theissen, G., *Urchristliche Wundergeschichten. Ein Beitrag zur formgeschichtlichen Erforschung der synoptischem Evangelien* (SNT 8), Gütersloh 1974.

Tilborg, S. van, *The Jewish Leaders in Matthew*, Leiden 1972.

Tillesse, G. Minette de , *Le secret messianique dans l'Evangile de Marc* (LD 47), Paris 1968.

Trilling, Wolfgang, *Das wahre Israel. Studien zur Theologie des Matthäus-Evangeliums* (SANT 10), München 1964.

Tödt, H. E., *Der Menschensohn in der synoptischen Überlieferung*, Gütersloh 1959.

Ulfgard, H., *Feast and Future. Revelation 7:9–17 and the Feast of Tabernacles* (ConBNT 22), Lund 1989.

VanderKam, James C., "The Righteousness of Noah", in: J. Collins–G. Nickelsburg (ed.), *Ideal Figures in Ancient Judaism. Profiles and Paradigms* (SBLSCS 12), Ann Arbor 1980, 13–32.

Vanhoye, Albert, "Longue marche ou accès tout proche? Le contexte biblique de Hébreux 3,7–4,11", *Bib* 49, 1968, 9–26.

Viviano, Benedict T., "Social World and Community Leadership: The Case of Matthew 23.1–12, 34", *JSNT* 39, 1990, 3–21.

Vögtle, Anton, *Das Evangelium und die Evangelien. Beiträge zur Evangelienforschung*, Düsseldorf 1971.

—, *Das Neue Testament und die Zukunft des Kosmos* (Komm. u. Beitr. z. A. u. N.T), Düsseldorf 1970.

—, *Der Judasbrief / Der 2. Petrusbrief* (EKKNT), Solothurn-Düsseldorf-Neu-kirchen/Vluyn 1994.

—, *Die 'Gretchenfrage' des Menschensohnproblems. Bilanz und Perspektive* (QD 152), Freiburg-Basel-Wien 1994.

Volz, Paul, *Die Eschatologie der jüdischen Gemeinde im neutestamentlichen Zeitalter nach den Quellen der rabbinischen, apokalyptischen und apokryphen Literatur dargestellt.* Tübingen 1934.

Walker, Rolf, *Die Heilsgeschichte im ersten Evangelium* (FRLANT 91), Göttingen 1967.

Weber, F., *System der Altsynagogalen Palästinischen Theologie aus Targum, Midrasch und Talmud,* Leipzig 1880.

Weiss, Hans-Friedrich, *Der Brief an die Hebräer* (MeyerK), Göttingen 1991.

Wenham, David, "Being 'Found' on the Last Day: New Light on 2 Peter 3.10 and 2 Corinthians 5.3", *NTS* 33, 1987, 477–479.

—, *The Rediscovery of Jesus' Eschatological Discourse* (Gospel Perspectives 4), Sheffield 1984.

Wiebe, Willi, *Die Wüstenzeit als Typus der messianischen Heilszeit.* Diss. Göttingen 1939. (Typed).

Wilcox, M., *The Semitisms of Acts*, Oxford 1965.

Wolff, H.W., *Joel and Amos* (Hermeneia), Philadelphia 1977.

Zahn, Theodor, *Das Evangelium des Matthäus* (Zahn Komm.), 4. Aufl., Leipzig-Erlangen 1922.

Zehnle, Richard F., *Peter's Pentecost Discourse. Tradition and Lukan Reinterpretation in Peter's Speeches of Acts 2 and 3* (SBLMS 15), Nashville-New York 1971.

Zeller, Dieter, "Die Bildlogik des Gleichnisses Mt 11,16f./Lk 7,31f.", *ZNW* 68, 1977, 252–257.

Zmijewski, Josef, *Die Eschatologiereden des Lukas-Evangeliums. Eine traditions- und redaktionsgeschichtliche Untersuchung zu Lk 21,5–36 und Lk 17,20–37* (BBB 40), Bonn 1972.

INDEX OF SCRIPTURAL PASSAGES

Old Testament

Gen
2:2 - 100
4:10 - 75
4:26 - 11
5:18–29 - 14
6:2 ff. - 106
6:2 f. - 11, 14
6:3 - 111
6:9 - 13, 57
7:1 - 18, 19, 57
9:2 - 94
14:13 - 12
19:4 ff. - 62
19:17 - 63
19:26 - 63
19:30–38 - 62

Ex
8:15 - 35
15:16 - 94
15:24 - 93
16:2 - 93
16:3 - 94
16:7 - 93
16:8 - 93, 95
16:9 - 93
16:12 - 93
16:35 - 98
17:1–7 - 23, 43
17:2 ff. - 15, 22
17:2 - 23, 43
17:3 - 23, 93
17:7 - 15, 23, 24, 43,
     55, 93, 94, 97
17:16 - 9
19:8 - 50
19:17 - 50, 64
23:20 - 39
24:7 - 48, 50
32 - 48, 49, 53
32:1 ff. - 51, 94

32:4 - 48
32:6 - 49
32:8 - 94
32:26 - 15
32:31 - 49

Lev
18 - 31

Num
11:1 - 93
11:4 ff. - 22
13:16 - 16, 89
14 - 99
14:2 - 93, 99
14:3–4 - 94
14:5 - 99
14:6 ff. - 99
14:7 - 99
14:11 - 43, 54, 94
14:19 - 99
14:22 - 15, 22, 23, 24,
     94, 99
14:23 - 43
14:24–30 - 15
14:24 - 95, 99
14:27 - 54, 93
14:29–31 - 99
14:29 - 15, 93
14:30 - 99
14:33–34 - 98
14:35 - 99
14:36 - 93
14:38 - 99
14:43 - 94
16:11 - 93
16:32 - 11
17:6 - 93
17:20 - 93
17:25 - 93
20:3 - 42
20:10 - 94
20:12 - 15
20:13 - 43, 97
20:24 - 43, 97

21:5 - 42, 94, 95
21:7 - 42, 94, 95
26:65 - 15
27:14 - 43, 97
32:12 - 15
32:13 - 14, 15, 98
34:17 - 15

Deut
1:35–38 - 15
1:35 - 8, 14, 19, 22, 25
2:7 - 98
2:25 - 94
4:35 - 50
6:16 - 23, 24, 97
9:7 - 94
9:22 - 97
9:24 - 94
18:15 - 22, 51
18:18 - 22
31:17 - 54
32:1 ff. - 50
32:4 - 95
32:5 f. - 44
32:5 - 8, 14, 15, 22, 40,
     47, 48, 53, 55, 89,
     92, 93, 95, 97
32:20 f. - 48
32:20 - 8, 14, 15, 26,
     47, 48, 53, 55, 95
32:28 f. - 44
32:51 - 43, 97
33:8 - 43, 97
33:21 - 16
34:10 f. - 22

Josh
9:18 - 92
14:1 - 15
21:43–45 - 99 f.
21:44 - 100

1 Kings
5:9–14 - 32
5:9 - 32